MEDIA STORIES
IN THE
FALKLANDS-MALVINAS CONFLICT

Lucrecia Escudero Chauvel

Critical, Cultural and Communications Press
Nottingham
2014

Media Stories in the Falklands-Malvinas Conflict, by Lucrecia Escudero Chauvel

The rights of Lucrecia Escudero Chauvel in this work have been asserted by her in accordance with the Copyright, Designs and Patents Act, 1988.

© Lucrecia Escudero Chauvel, 2014.

All unauthorised reproduction is hereby prohibited. This work is protected by law. It should not be duplicated or distributed, in whole or in part, in soft or hard copy, by any means whatsoever, without the prior and conditional permission of the Publisher, CCC Press.

First published in Great Britain by Critical, Cultural and Communications Press, 2014.

All rights reserved.

Cover design by Hannibal.

CONTENTS

Acknowledgments 7
Preface by Umberto Eco 9

THE MEDIA CONTRACT

Producing the News
Historical and Research Antecedents 15
What is the Nature of News Stories? 20
The Media Contract 23
The Emergence of Fictionality 24
Narrative Worlds and Small Media Worlds 25

The Fascination of War
Argentine Media Overview 28
The News Permeability Syndrome 31
The News "Malvinisation" Syndrome 36

The Print News Agenda During the War
The Schematic Nature of the News 38
News About the Malvinas-Falklands 41
A Quantitative Reading 46
The Strategic Use of Sources during War 47

Information Sources and News Production
Good and Bad Coverage? 51
Empirical and Textual Sources 54
Newspapers' Own Sources 55
National and International News Agency 57
Official Information: the Argentine Military Government 58
The Media as Sources 61
"What do All These Rumours Mean?" 63

THE CONSTRUCTION OF MEDIA TRUTH

Blackouts, Denials and Secrets
Revelations, Denials and Spies 75
Identity Problems 80
Personalisation and Depersonalisation 82
The Functionality of Sources 84
Trust and Credibility 86

The Life, Passion and Death of a Rumour
The Story of the *Superb* Submarine	88
The Proliferation of the Rumour	95
Altered States	96
The Death of the Rumour	100
Media Truth	101
Many Years Later	109

Acts of War
Information from the Front	110
Argentine Military's Stories	113
Just who are *Los Lagartos*?	116
What to do with Those Cumbersome Prisoners of War?	119
A Very Special Prisoner: The Case of Alfredo Astiz	121

Stories, Sinkings and Torpedoes
The War Chronicle	124
The Sinking of the ARA *General Belgrano*	127
The Sinking of the Sheffield	134

Epilogue
The Double Reader	141
The British Veto	146
"*With Eyes Filled with Tears*"	147
The Readers' Revenge	150

Conclusion: Constructing Memory
Falklands-Malvinas as Years Go By: From Epics to Anecdote	155
Historical Memory	155
Memory as an Intimate Chronicle Twenty Years On	158
The Role of the Media	160
Conclusions	162

Bibliography	164
Index	167

To Manuel Ernesto

Acknowledgments

This book was made possible thanks to various grants and scholarships. I would like to thank the Argentine National Council for Scientific Research (Consejo Nacional de Investigaciones Científicas de la República Argentina) whose foreign study scholarship allowed me to attend doctoral research seminars in semiotics at the University of Bologna under the supervision of Umberto Eco, who also kindly wrote the Preface to this edition.

I would like particularly to thank Professor Bernard McGuirk, who produced the most important and fruitful conferences and colloquia on this topic within the framework of post-conflict studies, and who created the Centre for the Study of Post-Conflict Cultures at the University of Nottingham. Since January 2003, and particularly at the colloquium of June 2004, in collaboration with the University of Bologna, I have had the invaluable opportunity to meet British researchers on this topic, which enabled me to update my research with the bibliography and the issues at stake in the current debates on the matter. But it was undoubtedly Bernard's bright and magical idea of organising the International Colloquium on "The Falklands-Malvinas Conflict Twenty-Five Years On" (November 2006) which made possible the most extraordinary and unprecedented meetings between officers and soldiers from both sides, and marked a turning point in how to approach this kind of research. The depth of the debate and the emotional charge of these encounters demonstrate how research work in the humanities and social sciences cannot leave out the human factor and the power of media stories.

Professor Paolo Fabbri, then at the University of Bologna, was immeasurably helpful in the initial phase of describing the media's sociological paradigms. His observations allowed me to tighten the theoretical frame around the information sources of the newspapers being studied. Discussions with Professor Greg Philo of the Glasgow Media Group were most stimulating and insightful.

Barrister Sophie Thonon, who fought to take to court those responsible for the bloody Argentine dictatorship, further enlightened me about the close links between the Falklands-Malvinas conflict and human rights. Mike Seear, officer of the Gurkha Regiment, and Argentine Counter-Admiral Carlos Hugo Robacio, who commanded the heroic BIM no. 5, showed me the high level of military professionalism and the courage necessary not only for fighting but also for reconciliation. This book is the result of these encounters and discussions.

I would also like to thank journalists Ricardo Kirschbaum, Oscar Raúl Cardoso and Horacio Vebitsky for their interest in this book and the information that they have contributed to it; Atilio Molteni, in charge of the Argentine Embassy in London at the time, for generously responding to my numerous questions; and Guillermo Olivera, of the University of Stirling, who patiently carried out the English translation.

Preface
Umberto Eco

A recent dissertation by scholar Lucrecia Escudero Chauvel, concerning the Argentine press's coverage of the Falklands-Malvinas war, contained the following story.

On 31 March 1982, two days before the Argentine landing in the Falklands-Malvinas and twenty-five days before the arrival of the British Task Force in the Falklands, the Buenos Aires newspaper *Clarín* published an interesting item: allegedly, a London source claimed that Britain had sent the *Superb*, a nuclear submarine, to the Austral area of the South Atlantic. The British Foreign Office said immediately that they did not have any comment on this "version" and the Argentine press inferred that, if the British authorities qualified the report as a "version", this meant someone had leaked serious and secret military information.

On 1 April, when Argentines were on the verge of landing in the Falklands-Malvinas, *Clarín* reported that the *Superb* was a ship of 45.000 tons, carrying a crew of ninety-seven specialists in scuba diving.

Subsequent reactions by the British were pretty ambiguous. A military expert said that sending nuclear submarines of the *hunter-killer* type to that region would have been reasonable. *The Daily Telegraph* gave the impression of knowing a lot about the whole business, and step by step the rumour became fact.

Argentine readers were shocked by the event, and the press tried to meet their narrative expectations by keeping them in suspense. The information it gave allegedly came directly from the Argentine military command, and the *Superb* became "that submarine which English sources locate in the South Atlantic". On 4 April the submarine had already been sighted not far from the Argentine coasts. British military sources continued to answer all questions by saying they had no intention of revealing the location of their submarines, and such an obvious statement reinforced the general opinion that there were English submarines somewhere – which, of course, was quite true.

Also on 4 April, several European press agencies reported that the *Superb* was on the verge of sailing toward the South Seas, at the head of the British Task Force. If this had been so, the submarine sighted near the Argentine coasts could not have been the *Superb,* but such a contradiction reinforced, rather than weakened, the submarine syndrome.

On 5 April the press agency DAN announced that the *Superb* was 250 kilometres from the Falklands-Malvinas. The rest of the media followed, describing all the characteristics of the submarine and its extraordinary power. On 6 April the Argentine navy spotted the vessel near the archipelago, and in the following week it was joined by a brother, the submarine Oracle. On 8 April, the French daily *Le Monde* mentioned the two ships, and *Clarín* quoted the French report under the dramatic title "A Submarine Fleet?" On 12 April the submarine fleet showed up again, and *Clarín* furthermore announced the arrival of Soviet submarines in southern waters.

Now, this story concerns not only the presence of the *Superb* (which was taken for granted) but also the diabolical abilities of the Britons, who succeeded in keeping their position secret. On 18 April a Brazilian pilot sighted the *Superb* near Santa Catarina and took a picture of it, but the image was blurred because of the cloudy weather. Here is yet another effect of fog, this time provided directly by readers in order to sustain the necessary suspense of the story. We seem to be halfway between *Flatland* and Antonioni's *Blow-Up*.

On 22 April, when the British Task Force was really eighty kilometres from the theatre of operations, with true warships and true submarines, *Clarín* informed its readers that the submarine which had allegedly been patrolling the Malvinas had returned to Scotland. On 23 April, the Scottish *Daily Record* revealed that, as a matter of fact, the *Superb* had never left its British base. Argentine newspapers were obliged to find another narrative genre, shifting from war movies to spy novels and, on 23 April, *Clarín* announced triumphantly that the deception of the British forces had been unmasked.

Who invented the Yellow Submarine? The British secret services, in order to lower the spirits of Argentines? The Argentine military command, in order to justify its tough stance? The British press? The Argentine press? Who benefited from the rumour? I am not interested in this side of the story. I am interested in the way the whole story grew out of vague gossip, through the collaboration of all parties. Everybody cooperated in the creation of the Yellow Submarine because it was a fascinating fictional character and its story was narratively exciting.

This story – that is, the real story of a fictional construction – has many morals. In the first place, it shows that we are continually tempted to give shape to life through narrative schemes. Second, it demonstrates the force of existential presuppositions. In every statement involving proper names or definite descriptions, the reader or listener is supposed to take for granted the existence of the entity about which something is predicated. If someone tells me that he was unable to attend a meeting because his wife was ill, my first reaction is to take for granted the existence of that wife. Only later, if by chance I discover that the speaker is a bachelor, can I conclude that he was lying through his teeth. But until that moment, because his wife has been *posited* within the discursive framework by the act of mentioning her, I have no reason to think she does not exist. This is such a natural inclination on the part of normal human beings that if I read a text beginning "As everyone knows, the present king of France is bald" (taking into account that France is generally known to be a republic and that I am not a philosopher of language but a normal human being), I do not start consulting the Truth Tables; rather, I decide to suspend my disbelief and take the discourse as a fictional one, which probably tells a story set in the time of Charles the Bald. I do this because it is the only way to assign a form of existence in whatever world to the entity posited by the statement.

Thus it happened with our submarine. Once posited by the discourse of the mass media, the submarine was there, and since newspapers are supposed to tell the truth about the actual world, people did their best to sight it.

In *Ma che cos'è questo amore* by Achille Campanile, that sublime comic writer, there is a character named Baron Manuel who, in order to facilitate his secret adulterous life, continually tells his wife and others that he is obliged to visit and assist a certain Pasotti, a dear friend of his, who is chronically ill and whose health tragically declines as Baron Manuel's love affairs become more and more complicated. The presence of Pasotti is so palpable in the novel that even though both the author and the reader know he does not exist, there comes a point when everybody (certainly the other characters, but also the reader) is prepared for him to appear physically on the scene. So Pasotti suddenly shows up, unfortunately a few minutes after Baron Manuel (who has become disgusted with his adulterous life) has announced Pasotti's death.

The Yellow Submarine was posited by the media, and as soon as it was posited everyone took it for granted. What happens when in a fictional text the author posits as an element of the actual world (which is the background of the fictional one) something that does not obtain in the actual world?

From *Six Walks in the Fictional Woods*
(Cambridge, MA: Harvard University Press, 1995).
Reproduced with the permission of the author.

The Media Contract

PRODUCING THE NEWS

Historical and Research Antecedents

Towards the end of 1982, during the presidency of General Emilio Bignone, who had taken over the government since the military defeat and resignation of General Fortunato Galtieri, a team of social science researchers began a qualitative study on Argentine political behaviours, beliefs and attitudes about the recent democratisation process that had been provoked by the defeat in the Malvinas-Falklands and the fall of the Military Junta that had led the operation.[1]

The method used by the researchers consisted of asking a series of general and open-ended questions: What did the subjects think about Argentina? What did they believe to be the most relevant political issues? How did they perceive the Argentine ruling class? In short: what did the Argentines think about their country and what did they expect from it?

I know of no other study from the period that directly addressed the effects of Argentina's political repression and the Malvinas-Falklands war on these segments of Argentine society, nor on the media's role in influencing their belief and opinions about the war. This study was the first to analyse and discuss the issue of the war in terms of the Argentine news press's legitimacy in the formation of public opinion. Its use of self-reporting measures about the short-term effects of a dramatic and highly political media event was significant.

When compared with another study, performed by EMI about the Malvinas-Falklands conflict, there are interesting findings. EMI carried out the first opinion survey about the war in April 1982, when the Malvinas-Falklands conflict was only a month old. The results of this study indicated that Argentines had a favourable opinion of the war: 88% of those surveyed believed that the war strengthened Latin-American relations, 79% wanted to employ the Inter American Defence Treaty (TIAR), 71% believed that the war would improve relations with the Soviet Union, 69% rejected the United Nations' proposal of an international peace-keeping force, and 65% were in favour of breaking through the British blockade. (*Clarín,* 17 April, "Public opinion during

---

[1] *Opiniones y creencias de los argentinos frente a las elecciones presidenciales de octubre de 1983* [Opinions and Beliefs of the Argentineans About the Presidential Elections in October 1983], Buenos Aires 1983 (mimeo). This study was one of the first investigations into the political marketing surrounding Radicalist Raul Alfonsin's presidential campaign.

the conflict").[2]

What, though, did the Argentines who were surveyed at the end of 1982 say? The three political events that they believed to be the most relevant to Argentina were: the *desaparecidos* [disappeared, missing people],[3] the Malvinas-Falklands war, and the economic crisis. Within these responses, the issue of those who had disappeared during the "dirty war" and the war with Great Britain had something in common aside from the shared themes of violence, destruction, and death. That something was, as one of the research participants put it, the feeling that "something was hidden from us". This quest for the truth and collective need for frankness became very important in the years following the recovery of democracy.

The study concluded that one of the effects of the military rule on Argentine society was the installation of a communications schema modelled on the military's internal communications system. This schema was composed of two elements, the harangue and the order, which by definition excluded the possibility of dissent or response. In the rituals of the military, it is imperative that soldiers, just like members of a militarised society, have only one possible narrative programme available to them, i.e. obedience, and that this response be established by only one acceptable speech act: the oath of loyalty (Escudero-Chauvel 1978).

The militarised communication style reached its zenith during the Malvinas-Falklands war. Its ultimate effect was the transformation of social subjects into "objects" who were directly impacted by an underlying belief system that failed to consider them as historical protagonists. A militarised social culture developed which gave military-

---

[2] The British public opinion surveys published weekly by *The Economist* indicated a high level of support for the Prime Minister's policy (Sergeant 1985). Other opinion polls, such as the ones carried out by *The Sunday Times*, indicated that at the beginning of May 70% of the British were in favour of the British military invasion of the island, 70% were satisfied with how the government was conducting the war, 18% thought that it was wiser to abandon the subject, while 11% were undecided. (Glasgow University Media Group 1985: 136-43). According to Max Hastings and Simon Jenkins, some surveys give the impression that public opinion was ambivalent to the war and that, although many were in favour of Task Force operations, they were not in favour of going to war. The nation seemed to be sure the British government would only simulate a war (Hastings and Jenkins 1983: 157).

[3] People who disappeared during the military regime and were believed to have been tortured and assassinated by the Armed Forces

type responses and which failed to revise the axiological content of these responses. As such, it was always "others" who spoke for Argentine society. This communicational impotence is perhaps best expressed in the words of one of the research participants: "We are like puppets whose strings are being badly manipulated."

The following year, in Argentina, RISK carried out a study which focused primarily on Argentine national concerns, but also examined Argentine attitudes towards foreign investment. The results of this investigation indicated that, only one year after the Malvinas defeat, the sovereignty of the islands ranked fifth in importance after political instability, inflation, unemployment and the high cost of living. 59% of those surveyed believed that "Foreigners can learn many things from the Argentines". A sense of national superiority was emerging during the period throughout all sectors of Argentine society. The idea of national superiority, despite the loss of the Malvinas, despite the economic crisis, and despite the lack of democracy, deviated from nationalism and embodied the element of ethnocentrism which was congruent with the most elementary data of Argentina's recent history at the time. The presence of ethnocentrism is an indicator of the pervasiveness of authoritarian tendencies in Argentine society.

In February of 1990, during Carlos Menem's presidency, diplomatic relations were re-established between Great Britain and Argentina. The diplomatic accord, which was signed in Madrid, specifically referred to a zone of Argentine military exclusion around the Malvinas-Falklands. This exclusion, however, did not prevent the Argentine government from stating that it had sovereignty over the islands in international fora, a claim which has been maintained by Argentina until the present.[4]

In March of 1990, one month after signing the accord, almost a decade after the Argentine landing on the Malvinas-Falklands, and practically seven years after the establishment of democratic rule in Argentina, a simultaneous survey was performed in Great Britain and Argentina at the request of the South Atlantic Council. In response to the question, "Which is the most important international problem to currently resolve?", the British ranked the Falklands-Malvinas in third place after international peace and Northern Ireland. The Argentines, on the other hand, felt that their country's greatest problem was foreign

---

[4] For example, in early June 2014, before commencing its 2014 World Cup finals campaign, the entire Argentine national football team was pictured in a packed La Plata stadium behind a banner reading "Las Malvinas Son Argentinas".

debt, followed by sovereignty over the Malvinas, and finally the integration of Latin America. The development and change in public opinion is significant in terms of the importance attributed to the Argentine democratisation process and its rising political stability. Subjects were asked if they felt that "the end of the military government and the success of democratic national elections in Argentina in 1983 produced a great difference, some difference or no difference in the possibility of reaching a final conciliation between Argentina and Great Britain?" The Argentine and British subjects gave the following responses:

	Argentina	Great Britain
A great difference	26%	13%
Some difference	34%	37%
No difference	22%	27%
No opinion	18%	23%

Table 1. Argentine and British opinions about the difference that Argentina's democratic elections had made in British-Argentine relations. Source: South Atlantic Council.

The social perceptions of 60% of the Argentines and 50% of the British surveyed were that the democratic regime had produced a difference in diplomatic relations. In terms of the Argentine responses, seven years of democratic rule in the country had most likely produced this change in public opinion.[5]

Looking at how news was circulated during the Malvinas-Falklands war is key to the study undertaken in this book. The issue of news circulation not only closes a complete chapter of Argentine discursive history, which can be entitled "the rise and fall of military discourse", but also and above all indicates that forms of news production, circulation and reception about this war were set into motion by a system of beliefs, endorsements and rejections which ultimately formed Argentine public opinion. In short, the transparency of this information

---

[5] For the cited study, see *La opinión pública argentina e inglesa ante la cuestión Malvinas* [The Argentine and British Public Opinion *vis-à-vis* the Falklands-Malvinas Question], Buenos Aires, March 1990 (mimeo). This transatlantic study on national issues was carried out by Mora, Araujo, Noguera and Associates (Argentina), and by Gallup (UK).

legitimised the political leadership, yet could consequently be negatively affected by the de-legitimisation of the media. In 1990 I carried out a qualitative study whose aim was to verify the ability of the media to construct an agenda which would fix the war memory, the so-called long term media effect, and the credibility given to the press. To the question "What does being well-informed mean?", research participants replied:

"I was well informed about what was supposed to be known, but the turn of events showed me that I was not well informed. The war happened far away and we were being pressured by nationalism. What could we do?" (Andres V., age 38, businessman)

"I found out about both the Mothers in the Plaza de Mayo and the concentration camps when I was in Paris for the 1978 World Cup. There, I realized that the information we had been receiving was misinformation. And in 1982, the same thing happened again." (Alfredo P., age 43, pilot)

"I think that even if the dirty war was much more serious as an event and much more perverse as a function, it was still through the Malvinas war that Argentine society became aware that the military institution was degenerating, that its methods were perverse and that its ideas were anachronisms." (Germán G., age 43, architect)

"I knew that the war was inside of Argentina and that what had to be saved were the Argentine soldiers and not the British ones. Fear had already been planted. It was as though the defeat was what led us back to democracy." (Alicia C, age 41, union leader)

"In the beginning, during the first days, I believed in the national press, until I started to detect a contradiction between it and the BBC and began to wonder if they (the Argentine press) were doing the same thing as they'd done with the dirty war. This suspicion became stronger for me when the fighting started." (Horacio V., journalist)

The mediatisation process that Argentine society underwent during the war and the later presidential campaigns of 1983, indicate that the country quickly moved from a representational system based on media dependence (i.e. the idea that the press is there to tell us the truth) to a media "truth" production system that appears to have been strongly interdependent with the political sphere. The breadth of this representational transformation also runs from Raúl Alfonsín's 1983 presidential campaign, which was still rooted on the format of "denouncing" a secret pact and promising social transparency, to Carlos Menem's 1989 campaign, which based itself on the economic crisis and used television as a political medium.

If political systems are at least partly sustained by particular narrative systems that imbue them with historical intelligibility, then the news media play the most important role in this dynamic by virtue of their widespread and heterogeneous production and circulation of contemporary stories. This comprehensibility signals the limits between the true and the non-true. A narration that is untrue can become more than true in political language games: it can be elevated to the level of "objective truth". There are other narrations which refuse directly to label themselves as true or untrue; they base their structure on this haziness (e.g. the case of rumours). Recent Argentine history offers several examples of this type of narration, including those circulated about the war and the disappeared (Escudero-Chauvel, 2000, 2002a, 2002b). Media societies, which are both hyper-realistic and hyper-imaginary, go beyond truth and non-truth because these societies are immersed in enigmatic appearance reversals.

What appears to me to be fundamental is that all narrations, whatever their meaning, have an active potential and material power to produce effects: to be accepted, rejected, consumed, believed to be true, untrue, or uncertain. The narration simply sticks. There is no such thing as a completely "true" narration or a completely "untrue" one, instead there are narrative systems which are put into circulation and later fixed, during a specific moment of social semiosis, in order to be recognised as true – or untrue – under particular consumption conditions. Once again, that which is in play is a complex interaction between a system of beliefs and a system of emotions.

What Is the Nature of News Stories?

Narrative can be ascribed to the news genre, and not the literary or fictional one, when a match exists between the narrated propositions and extra-discursive events. Certainly, any media consumer knows that the concept of truth is suspicious. The perception of a real world, or "empirical world", is not independent of both discursive functioning and the thought and value systems of the audiences. American philosopher Hilary Putnam argues this point in his discussion of the concept of "truth". For Putnam, truth is not a simple concept. The idea that truth is simply a passive reproduction of something that really exists has been discredited. Noting that the very concept of transcendental correspondence of our representations with the real world has no meaning, the philosopher argues that we have now been deprived of the old realist idea of a corresponding truth (Putnam 1985: 140, 146, 149).

In media land, the truth is always discursive: it is the result of coinciding stories, alternating and contrasting versions of these stories, denials and declarations, to cite a few of the verification criteria internal to the profession. The press's narrative systems, however, have the paradoxical powers of circulating "untrue" statements – in the sense of occurred/not occurred events – whose immediate effect is that of presenting the truth without empirically verifying it. In summary, *the truth is an effect of discourse.*

Although it may seem self-apparent, I will attempt to demonstrate that there is not a "single" narration about the Falklands-Malvinas war, but rather a multiplicity of stories and narrative voices; that which places the news system into circulation is the construction of *possible worlds*. These worlds create an interpretative repertoire that closes when the news media decides to withdraw a particular world from its agenda. The interpretative possibilities are infinite as they are made of continuous feedback loops that exist from media to media, from newspaper section to newspaper section, from source to source, from day to day, and from rumour to rumour.

A centralist or centripetal viewpoint is dispersed when one analyses the news discourse. The construction of sources as being internal functions of the media story, the alternation and interplay of different press genres, the contrast of different enunciative positions such as witness, commentator, expert, etc., and the circulation of rumours, i.e. unverified information, shows the complexity and heterogeneity of the press's strategies and the kind of relationship that it attempts to establish with its readers. At the same time, though, the analysis of the construction of "public events", which we more commonly call "the news", shows to what extent the genre is rigid, conventional and repetitive. Like other products of mass culture, the news media try to display a pedagogical truth device for the reader, who will have to recognise it, fill it in, interpret it, and form conjectures about it.

The story of the Malvinas-Falklands war that was constructed by the Argentine news media reveals a proto-media society in the process of becoming increasingly mediatised. Its proto-mediatisation is apparent, given the fact that the debate about the veracity or falseness of the information transmitted during the period is still being waged: what continued in play after the war was the issue of sticking to the facts. What is truly interesting about this issue is what the media narration brings to light, i.e. the moment at which the political regime and the media explicitly placed themselves in the institutional position of "producing the truth". It is at this moment that the problem of reality construction forms emerge and this problem is a classic one in narrative theory, media studies and professional journalistic deontology.

You, the reader, may now rightfully be asking yourself what it is that makes the news discourse different from other types of discourses. "Once upon a time there was a queen" is completely different from "Yesterday, the Queen of England decided" as, among other things, the reader can think, "I'm dealing with a fairy tale" with the first fragment, and infer that "I'm reading a news story" with the second. The question, however, remains salient: how does a reader ascribe a fictional possible world to the first statement, and the possibility of factual possible world to the second?

The news industry does not produce a homogenous discourse. In fact, what is generally labelled "the news discourse" is an *umbrella* concept that results from a conjunction of different levels and complex heterogeneous enunciation operations. The news discourse appears to be filled with a referential function whose objective is to *let know*. In the case of the written press, the objective of this letting know is the construction of what Roland Barthes calls *l'illusion réferetielle* [refential illusion] (1984). At first glance, this construction appears to present the news as a neutral surface. As such, the voice of the journalist seems at one with a strategy of presenting the facts, just as the omniscient narrator is hardly noticed in realist novels. This dynamic seems to strengthen another of the press's ideological operations, concealing cracks in the news discourse by presenting the reader with a water-tight legitimacy and comprehensibility. Other media forms, such as television, can and do use a different manifestation system in which production traces are accentuated (e.g. expressions such as "we are receiving this information just now", which are absent from the print news discourse). In the construction of this verisimilitude, the description of actors and places, and the specification of dates, times and amounts, play the role of giving the story objectivity. I do not believe that these elements alone constitute the discriminating factor that marks the newspaper genre, but rather that they are a constant which spans all news discourse. Roland Barthes' question about the narration of events placed under the imperious guarantee of "the real" is structurally different from that directed towards imaginary or fictional narration. In the case of media stories, we can find these objectivity indicators in the systematic mention of sources, places or temporality that are one of the privileged forms of media narration. This strategy poses the media as an historically impartial "outsider" who "listens" to information and then repeats it (i.e. the reflectionist theory of the media), just like the historian.

The Media Contract

While history's status is uniformly assertive and verifiable, the status of the news is independent from its contents, that may or may not have happened, but relies on persuading us that they did. In the words of a British correspondent covering the Malvinas-Falklands war:

> I definitely take the view that the British public is sufficiently sophisticated to detect Argentine lies quite easily. I think it is also important that we should understand what is happening on the other side [...] When we speak the truth because we are the BBC, this actually helps the Government. Why are our figures about Harrier losses believed? It's because Brian Hanrahan said "I saw them take off and I saw the same number land" – that's what we went around the world with and everybody believed it. (*The Observer*, 16 May 1982)

The status of both historical discourse and news discourse is fundamentally constative and assertive, which gives it a specific weight: it is a discourse of Being, in which all doubt appears only on rare occasions. George Howard's statements about the controversy that exploded in the British and Argentine press, about the accuracy of both sides' information on one of the many air battles, shows to what extent the legitimacy of the press is consolidated not only by its, but also by the news's, vocation to "speak the truth".

I propose calling the particular form of fiduciary contract that the news tries to establish with its readers *the media contract*. In this contract, audiences implicitly accept as truthful the narration channelled by the news and leave the possibility of eventual verification as virtual. Consequently, they give the news media not only a legitimacy that is based on the institution which the media represents, but also a trust which has to do with the inter-subjective bond that links the media with their audiences. That is why the information crises (blackouts, lies, false interviews or reports, etc.) are so serious.

The media contract has a cooperative nature, but above all a credit-giving one. It serves as an anterior frame to the development, actualisation and recognition of the newspapers' enunciative strategies. As such, it has an eminently fragile nature because it permanently runs the risk of being broken by discreditation.

Summing up, it is intrinsic for the media contract to give the narrative of the factual world a privileged "real" meaning, and simultaneously a "true" one. Classic research on the production of the news and its routines centred on the study of the criteria of news worthiness, and the transformation of "fact" into an event that earns the status of "news", shows not only the restrictions and rituals which news producers submit themselves to, but, above all, the processes required to reach the construction of an illusion: that of media "truth".

The Emergence of Fictionality

We have already seen how the large scale production of legitimisation mechanisms is characteristic of the news genre, such as the reference to information sources or the alternation of organisational and testimonial "framing". On the one hand, it is in the organisation of this true narrative topic, that of "telling the truth", that we can find the media's strength as a social institution. On the other hand, in a reception situation, consuming information is possible because of the media contract's credit-giving nature. This nature allows the audience to confer different levels of credibility to the media, thus corresponding to the narrative topic of "speaking the truth", which allows the audiences to distinguish between different types of newspapers (e.g. broadsheet and tabloid press) and television genres (docudrama, TV documentaries, television news, etc.).

It seems apparent that, in terms of its being a social contract, the media contract is basically stable and it is this stability that permits the circulation and consumption of news in the contemporary world without clamorous cases of communication collapse being verified. Crisis situations, such as wars or 9/11, are the limit cases that put the truthful nature of this contract to the test and permit it to advance in a theoretical direction. The news does not function very differently from "fiction" as both attempt to construct possible narrative worlds from descriptions of individuals who have their own programmes and courses of action.

While the fictional discourse articulates itself on intra- and extra-textual conventions that alert the reader to the fact that he or she is dealing with a fictional text even if it includes historical facts (as is often the case with historical novels), the news media attributes itself the power to state what is real even though it may include fictional elements, i.e. those which did not necessarily happen. It is precisely because of the media contract that audiences regularly consider real the fictional stories which appear in the news media. An interesting problem that the media contract presents is not only marking the frontier between the historical Napoleon and a docudrama's Napoleon (this has been one of the criteria used to distinguish history from historical fiction), but to see how the news media, assuming the presentation of some Napoleons, have the power to create fictional characters as ontological, corresponding to a certain world state. In all cases, the contract reveals not only news's basically interactional nature, but also the perception and relevance frames that the press proposes to the reader. Classical ethno-methodological media research (Fishman 1980; Tuchman 1978; Lester 1980) in this direction indicates that "News is a product of reality-making activities and not simply reality-describing ones" (Lester 1980: 984).

The possibility that it is the news which organises one of the modes of perceiving and experiencing the factual world implies that those images placed into circulation "are real in their consequences". One can perceive only that which has been previously staged by the media and Fishman postulates the category of "non-events" to highlight those which can only be perceived within a particular interpretative frame: "Implicitly, the notion of non-events includes at least two schemes of interpretation: one which leads an individual to see something, and one which leads an individual not to see something. As such, the concept is relational, it refers to a discontinuity between two perspectives" (Fishman 1980: 80).

Narrative Worlds and Small Media Worlds

War stories and the war of information reveal to what extent the media contract is the product of high textual technology. They also prove that the press normally operates through the construction of possible media worlds placed into circulation by the papers and that it is probably all media communication that obeys what Umberto Eco calls "small worlds" (1990). Eco affirms that "The narrative suggests that our vision of the real world may be as imperfect as that of the narrative characters" (1990: 204). In his recent analysis of the narrative procedures of fiction, he states that "Narrative worlds are parasites of the real world" (1994: 101). Extending the concept of possible worlds from narrative worlds to the media universe is useful because it allows us simultaneously to look at the different systems in which the news discourse transforms the factual world into a plausible story, that is, the news format as a narrative strategy.

As in the possible narrative world, the possible media world gives its readers a group of simplified and stereotypical frames which presuppose selection, interpretation and assembly processes. In this sense, the possible media world is also parasitic because the properties of the information objects it proclaims are not explained. They are left as such since the reader takes them for granted as existing in the "real" world.

It is possible that the audiences know very little about war technology, but take the information given by the consumed newspaper or television programme as valid. Through the parasitic effect, the reader inscribes this information into the totality of the possible world delineated as "war" and thereby constructs his or her own media encyclopaedia. As such, the different possible media worlds placed into circulation during the Malvinas-Falklands war are "small worlds" constructed by crossing newspaper information, which is by nature and definition fragmented – as is the encyclopaedia that the reader progressively forms about the war, in which equally coexist the "Argentine landing", "British blockade", "air war", and so on.

The story of the rumour of the nuclear submarine *Superb* or the landing of British troops on the Georgia Islands, which I shall analyse in the following chapters, are excellent examples of possible media worlds that appear to be veri-simile and, as such, credible, or even conceivable, to the reader. In the context of the possible world of "war", and in the act of forming his or her own encyclopaedia, the reader, who is backed by a conjunction of propositions and supported by the media contract that he or she has established with the newspaper, can deem that the deployment of a British nuclear submarine or an Argentine resistance on the Georgia Islands is not just "necessary", but even "possible". The fact that the information about the *Superb* and the Georgia Islands was later revealed to be fabricated not only fails to remove verisimilitude from these small worlds' construction, but does not even put the media contract into crisis. It is true, though, that the adding up of these small worlds eventually ended the political legitimacy of an entire government.

The recurrent presence of rumours in the press about the Malvinas-Falklands war demonstrates that news can be, and often is, a crazed machine that puts completely contradictory and simultaneous messages into circulation. These messages are independent from each other not only in terms of their truth conditions, but, above all, in terms of their use and verification conditions. I propose calling this *the immune deficiency information hypothesis*. According to this hypothesis, the presence of one crazed cell is sufficient to destroy an entire system normally immune to lies. For this reason, it seems important to me to distinguish between the newspaper's production routines, i.e. their strategies, and what readers do with these products.

In effect, circulated information is much more "false" – in the inaccurate or approximate sense of the term – than the reader would want, but he or she still accepts and consumes it as truthful. The basis of media truth's construction is the alternation of a two-fold pact between information readers and producers: an internal pact about the production of a discourse that is, at the least, verisimilar, and an external pact about the reception of this discourse during which its verification is generally impossible.

The media contract presupposes that at least one of these two systems attempts to construct a referential structure in which complex verisimilitude operations are mounted through the localisation, details or identification of the social actors involved and their actions. Neither of these two systems, however, needs to have a relationship with the "real", but only with what the reader presumes, wants, or believes to be "real", in other words, with the audience's system of expectations and beliefs. In situations of news information crises, such as wars, censorship, anti-censorship or information blackouts, these two pacts considerably distance themselves from each other and narrations become, at the very least, undecidable and non-imputable. Placing these two systems into relation with each other, what the Media Contract does, is to articulate the production of a narrative object – that we commonly call "the news" – with a system of beliefs, in other words, a system of an emotional nature.

THE FASCINATION OF WAR

Argentine Media Overview

Published works about the Malvinas-Falklands conflict, most of which date from 1982-86, are primarily focused on the narration of the war's development. This narration was, at the very least, created by its protagonists, who tended to focus on the war's technical military aspects, its repercussions on Latin American, European, and US diplomatic relations, or on the historical antecedents and validity and quality of the Argentine and British titles of possession to the islands.[1] British and European texts about the war highlight the strenuous and extensive debate that took place in Great Britain about the role, use and censorship of the press (Harris 1983; Adams 1986; Morrison and Tumber 1988; House of Commons Defence Committee 1982; Glasgow University Media Group 1985; Sergeant 1985, 1987, 1989; Holland 1982). During the nineties, research about identity, culture and nationalisms – in both countries – were predominant, and gave a new perspective to the war (Aulich 1992; Chambers 1993; Monaghan 1998; Foster 1999). In a more recent update, the monumental work of Sir Lawrence Freedman (2005) provides a very thorough historical synthesis. British Major Mike Seear's war journal (2003) and his later retrospective *Return to Tumbledown* (2012), as well as the meticulous account from the frontline by Argentine Counter-Admiral Carlos Hugo Robacio (re-edited in 2004) weave stories of contrasting views. Diego Garcia Quiroga's and Mike Seear's compilation puts together veterans' testimonies and researchers' studies in a synthesis that re-examines the conflict twenty-five years on (2007).

1982 data shows that 78% of Britons read at least one national newspaper daily. This percentage, one of the highest in Europe, rises to 85% when one includes the Britons who also purchased at least one regional newspaper. Sales figures indicate that the British press sold 14 million national newspapers daily in 1982 (18 million including Sunday editions) and 7 million regional papers (Sergeant 1989: 9). Argentine data from the same period shows similar trends. IPSA found that 77% of the population read national newspapers and 59.7% read weekly

---

[1] For an overview of Argentina's historical position concerning titles of possession to the Malvinas-Falklands islands, see Beach (1982) and Van Sant Hall (1983). In particular, see Gamba (1986: 23-62), which presents a solid historical-diplomatic documentation of the conflict concerning possession of the islands.

news magazines during the war. In terms of the written press, the Argentine public was basically an informed one. The national newspapers in this study were *Clarín* and *La Nación,* with daily editions of 500,000 and 230,000 to 250,000 respectively. *Clarín* also had a Sunday edition which reached 1,600,000 readers.

In terms of television and radio information, 20 million British households possessed a television in 1982 and were able to receive the two major public channels, BBC1 and BBC2, as well as a commercial channel, ITV. The findings of Sergeant's study indicate that Britons spent an average of three hours a day watching television and two and half hours a day listening to the radio (Sergeant 1989: 9). During the war, BBC1 and BBC2's television and radio news programmes had the largest audiences, followed by those of ITN (International Television News) and IRN (Independent Radio News). Beyond these stations' general programming, those transmissions specifically focused on the war with the highest level of viewers were ITN's *News at Ten,* with 17 million viewers the day that the Argentines surrendered on the Georgia Islands, followed by BBC1's *Nine O'Clock News.* ITN provided a special half hour news programme dedicated to the war entitled *The Falklands Special* and the BBC included a special section about the conflict in its *TV Eye.* The most controversial programme broadcast during the period was undoubtedly the BBC's *Panorama* (Adams 1986: 49, 51, 59).

During the month of March 1982, the Argentine viewing public preferred to watch football (28.4%) and two soap operas (27.2% and 24.5%) (IPSA: 1982), with broadcasts occupying the first three places in viewing choices during April. However, this trend changed completely as the public focused its attention on the state channel's news programmes.[2] An analysis of the type of programme and channels watched during the month of April 1982 indicates the following :

Channel	Time	Programme	Type	Rating
7	9-10pm	*60 Minutes*	News magazine	39.4%
13	8-10pm	*Good-Evening Argentina*	News	35.2%
11	2-3pm	*Mariana*	Soap Opera	34.6%
13	1-2pm	*Reality 82*	News magazine	33.8%

Table 2

[2] In Argentina, there is only one nationally transmitted television station, ATC Channel 7. Principal television stations, such as Channel 11 and Channel 13, were essentially controlled by the military after the 1976 coup.

In May, programme and channel choices were segmented as follows:

Channel	Time	Programme	Type	Rating
National	9-10.30pm	*First combats*	News magazine	59.6%
Chanel 7	9-10pm	*60 Minutes*	News magazine	44.0%
Chanel 11	2-3pm	*Mariana*	Soap Opera	43.6%
Chanel 7	9-11pm	*World Cup*	Football	37.5%

Table 3

From Saturday, 20 May to Sunday, 21 May, ATC broadcast "24 hours for the Malvinas". A telethon including the country's principal television figures, it was dedicated in solidarity to Argentine soldiers in the Malvinas. It reached an audience of 31.2 million people. The state channel also broadcast "To England with Humour", which satirised the British secret service. The month's programming closed with Channel ll's weekly Saturday night (8:30pm to 10pm) tribute to examples of Latin American solidarity, "Argentina, you aren't alone."

In the month of June, practically on the eve of the Argentine surrender, Pope John Paul II's visit reached the second rating place with 42.3% (12 June). In the month of July, with the war now over, news broadcasts fell to ninth place and comedy programmes rose in ratings to occupy the first three viewing spot places with rating levels of 35.3%, 32.1%, and 29.1%. News transmissions on Radio Belgrano, Radio Continental, Radio Mitre, Radio Splendid and Radio Nacional reached average ratings of 18 to 16% during the same time period (IPSA 1982).

Two levels of analysis allowed me to choose the material for this study. The first level had a descriptive and taxonomic nature that led to exposing the press's own journalistic visibility or "history according to the media" by studying newspaper sections and pagination. This internal taxonomy of the press yields both a reference and a title differentiation system. Later, the criteria of Malvinas-Falklands news and the construction of the newspapers' agendas presents a principle of basically differentiated themes. This first level of analysis is presented in Part One of this book.

The second level of analysis has to do with the organisation of global representation, "the war in the Malvinas-Falklands as narrated by the media", by working from the procedures placed in relief and created by the press. These procedures are similar to the classic narrative categories of Aristotelian rhetoric, such as the unity of action, place, time and theme. This level of analysis points then to the confrontation between the *narratio* elements in Argentine national dailies. The result of this comparison demonstrates homogenous properties that reveal the strategies placed on the textual scene by each particular newspaper. This analysis is presented in Part Two.

The news permeability syndrome
Even though it may appear premature to discuss the types of meaning effects that segmentation and integration procedures have on reception, I would still like to suggest an hypothesis that I call "the news permeability syndrome". According to this hypothesis, the quasi-totality of the news in the newspapers analysed is directly related to the conflict. Since the war overlapped sections and pseudo-sections, the reader could not find a "neutral space" in the paper that did not discuss the event. Even such a classic section as "Cattle Market" in *La Nación* reminds us that Argentines are at war by its reported fluctuation in beef prices.

An immediate effect of this syndrome is the dissemination of views and information on the conflict in such a way that the reader finds him or herself practically "imprisoned" by the discourse about the war. This syndrome is constant in Argentina's two principal daily newspapers, *Clarín* and *La Nación*. Simultaneously, whether it be on the content dimension of topics or on the formal plane of their expression, the news universe mirrors the social functioning and reinforces it. An exhaustive analysis of each newspaper will allow me to organise discussion of the news stories' segmentation network.

Clarín
Clarín is the most widely diffused national newspaper in Argentina. As we saw earlier, its circulation during the war – which is not highly different from its current diffusion – reached 500,000 copies a day. Its Sunday edition, which included a general theme magazine, sold 1,600,000 copies. *Clarín* has a tabloid format with a central body that oscillates between 50 and 60 pages. Articles appear in an integral form and are never fragmented nor continued on later pages except with rare exceptions. The newspaper's internal organisation is based on sections and sub-sections. These sections remained stable during the war. In order of appearance during the Malvinas-Falklands conflict they were: the front page, politics, economy, opinion, international news, general news.

La Nación

With its large format, *La Nación* had a smaller circulation during the war than did *Clarín*. It averaged between 230,000 to 250,000 daily editions along with a magazine and book supplement in its Sunday editions. The daily paper included a general news section, two classified ad columns, sports and diverse articles. Its central body averaged approximately 23 to 25 pages. The first section, general news, was considered to be the paper's principal body, as practically all news about the Malvinas-Falklands conflict was reported in its 15 to 20 pages.

In contrast to *Clarín*, *La Nación* does not appear to be highly sectioned. It is possible, however, to find a relative division in its news distribution. News about international politics, for example, always occupies the first few pages and is immediately followed by national political news. Another constant is an exclusively graphic one which serves to situate stories thematically: small sections are presented on the upper left hand side of the page with titles such as "Greater Buenos Aires" or "The Provinces". These titles indicate the geographical origin of the stories.

Within the pages of the paper's principal section, there is no apparent news hierarchy. Highly diverse stories coexist simultaneously. The absence of news hierarchy and sections contrasts with the presentation of news concerning agriculture and the beef industry. With sub-sections such as "Cattle", "Bulls", "Hogs", and "Livestock sales", the newspaper's internal world leads readers rapidly to situate news of interest to agricultural and livestock sectors who form *La Nación*'s traditional readers.

The only sections that can be identified by a stable placement and graphic indicators are the "Editorial", two signed opinion columns, and "Letters from Our Readers", all found on the centre pages. "Social Notes" – a sort of notebook of high society daily marriage and death notices, practically non-existent in *Clarín*, occupies a place of honour in *La Nación*. *La Nación*'s main body central format, with its weak hierarchy geared to a public which recognises pages of particular interest without specific sections, radically changed at the end of the 1980s. These changes and the profuse inclusion of new photographic and graphic materials were made in an attempt to modernise the paper, which was perceived as rather antiquated.

As it is easy to note, *Clarín* appears to have been both highly structured and to have had a strong sense of news hierarchy during the Malvinas-Falklands conflict period. A preponderance of national and international political news filled its agenda. In contrast, *La Nación* appears to have been highly structured only on its opinion and agriculture-livestock pages. It did not present any hierarchy in its internal organisation, not even in its reports of political news. If we compare the two newspapers' external visibility systems, we can draw two logics from a group of constants and differences:

	La Nación	*Clarín*
Number of Sections	>2	>2
Number of Pages	25-35	50-60
First Section number of pages	15-20	30-40
Internal classification	weak	high
Stable diagramming	weak	high
Hierarchisation	weak	high
Front page news articles	present	absent
Fragmented news articles	present	absent

Table 4

These marked differences become most pertinent across the three structural conditions that *Clarín* and *La Nación* manifest in the way they publish the news concerning the war. When compared to their British counterparts:

1. Both Argentine newspapers published special editions about Argentine forces landing of 2 April on the Malvinas-Falklands, as did the British press.
2. The Argentine newspapers did not modify their internal structure with special sections concerning the war. This means that, from the conflict's beginning, *Clarín* and *La Nación* refused to rupture textually their traditional news presentations systems in order to cover the war. In contrast, the majority of British papers immediately constructed a news category specific to the conflict.
3. The Argentine papers chose a diffused news presentation strategy for the war which longitudinally and transversally crossed all sections, thereby producing the effect of "the imprisoned reader" and the news permeability syndrome with which we have characterised this strategy. The British papers, as a result of their strong news categories, clearly produced a contrary effect, in which the reader was free to circulate within general news stories and could decide if they wanted to read those news items concerning the war.

To conclude this rapid panorama of the general news organs to which the Argentine reader had access, we should include the weekly news magazines of the time. The most important and largely distributed news magazines in Argentina were: *Revista Diez*, *Actualidad en familia*, and *La Semana y Usted*, edited by Editorial Perfil; *Revista Gente y la Actualidad* by Editorial Atlántida and *Siete Dias*, published by Editorial Abril. The circulation in the analysed time period was 23,000-25,000 for *Gente y la Actualidad* and *Siete Dias*, and 13,000-15,000 for *La Semana y Usted* and *Revista Diez*.

The Perfil Editorial group was created in the 1970s. It publishes for a particular market primarily composed of the middle (*La Semana*) and working classes (*Revista Diez*). These magazines, which earned an increasingly larger readership, compete for first place with two magazines put out by the weekly news publishers who have operated in Argentina since the middle of the century, Ediciones Atlántida.

The four weeklies present – and still maintain – common characteristics of the so-called "weekly news magazine": colourful covers with a large photo format and more than two titles, and an interior body filled with illustratively captioned images and 1-4 page articles. The internal agenda is generally constituted by articles written by special correspondents and reporter teams. Very few articles are picked up from foreign magazines. As such, material is based on national sources.

As with *La Nación*, these weekly magazines suffer from an absence of sections that organise internally presented material, as do *La Nación*, the editorial opinion columns in *La Semana*, *Gente* and *Siete Dias*. During the conflict, *Gente* presented additional sections that did not form part of its established format. These sections were "People", devoted to captioned photographs about the activities of show-business, political and sporting celebrities.

Unlike the national newspapers' lack of rupture with traditional presentation systems, the four magazines regularly published external captions and internal logos indicating special issues and news items about the conflict:

1. For ten issues including news about the war, *Gente* included a caption in its cover's upper right-hand corner indicating a "Special Issue". Given that the war began on Wednesday 30 March, the magazine was able to put the conflict on its Friday 1 April cover (no. 871). It also gave a captioned commentary of the war's final outcome in its 1 July edition (no. 884). Only these two issues about the beginning and end of the event were edited

with the identifying "Special Issue" cover captions. *Gente* magazine internally differentiated news dedicated to the conflict with a rectangular logo indicating the date of the Argentine landing and an image of the Malvinas-Falklands islands under the Argentine flag. This internal identification did not change during the time period and was summarised with article captions elevated to the category of news categories: "In a state of war", "The Georgia Battle", "We are winning!", "May's heroes", etc. It should be noted that the amount of space *Gente* dedicated to the war accounted for 90% of its total output.

2. *Revista Diez*'s internal logo was designed to resemble a stamp in which a group of soldiers hoisted an Argentine flag with the inscription "Malvinas Islands". This logo, however, was not consistent and often became confused with the article's title.

3. *La Semana* did not have external captions, but did have a single internal one which marked both the magazine's and public's opinions of what the outcome of the war should be: "*La Semana* at the front lines of victory". This caption included the visually represented news-agency telex.

4. *Siete Dias* did not present any auxiliary textual markers on either its exterior or interior. It did create a logo to indicate brief news items about the war which was composed of a square containing a map of the islands. The word "Telex" was written over the islands, thereby making a reference to a typical product within the news profession itself.

These weekly news magazines' internal and external graphic characteristics are sufficiently pertinent to map out an initial elementary functioning system that differentiates them:

	Siete Dias	*Gente*	*La Semana*	*Revista Diez*
External caption	+	-	+	-
Internal caption	+	+	+	-
Internal logo	+	-	+	+

Table 5

Unlike the two major Argentine newspapers, whose internal and external organisation did not change during the war, the Argentine news magazines each put a graphic and thematic device in motion in order to focus on particular aspects of the conflict. As such, the analysis of these magazines – from *Gente* and *Revista Diez* with their plentiful structural signs and indications about the conflict, to *Siete Dias*, which lacked external signs, but contained a large amount of internal information dedicated to the war – points to the fact that the general news genre underwent a large-scale change. Weekly general news magazines were transformed into real devices that graphically focused and set a scene for the war. This was done as an attempt to rival the televised press's presentational superiority and, above all, to offer the reader something that the news of the time rarely presented in the two enemy countries: images.

The weekly news magazine's centralisation of a single event allows the formulation of an hypothesis complementary to the daily press's news permeability syndrome. Argentine news magazines generally functioned within the written press system as producers of an immediate and non-ephemeral visibility about the conflict. At the same time, they became spokesmen of questions that the average reader had about the actors, settings and political and military mechanisms involved. In other words, onw witnessed the figurativisation of the news and the entire figurativisation of the war. In this sense, Argentine news magazines functionally resembled the British press's popular daily newspapers.

The news "Malvinisation" syndrome

The newspapers' news permeability syndrome is complementary to the weekly news magazine's news "Malvinisation" syndrome, according to which all information that passes through the weekly press reveals the machinery set into motion in the discourse about the war. In effect, the abundance of external and internal signs – logos, captions – as much as ostentatious indices, mark not only the reading forms being produced (adhesion, confidence, etc.), but above all an angle from which to read the presented material in a semantically created water-tight universe. Weekly magazines supported the Malvinas-Falklands war and expressed this support by giving it maximum visibility in their internal and external agendas and by transforming their entire presentation systems.

I believe that these two initial interpretative hypotheses, which are of course highly general and exclusively address the format set into operation in the written press's discourse, are complementary because they contribute to the production of the same effects. The effect is the "imprisoned" reader, who can neither escape nor subtract him or herself from a thematically coherent and graphic universe, because a neutral space literally does not exist. The overall society was supposed to be mobilised for war, and the press "reflected" this mobilisation in its structure.

As in all global events that shake a society, intensity and duration do not matter. In wars, terrorist attacks, earthquakes, presidential assassinations or royal weddings, to cite just some of the more classic example of the press's actual sagas, the written press is there to report the event. In the case of Argentina, however, the force and power of the story managed to contaminate practically the whole thematic universe, in the case of the newspapers, and the entire graphic-thematic universe, in the case of news magazines. In this way, a reader who cannot escape the fascination that the war produced in the press begins to be delineated.

Just what, though, did the Argentine press talk about during the war? Before addressing the issue of using news sources in war situations and the different enunciative strategies available for constructing the narrations placed into circulation by the press, I will call the reader's attention to the coherence of the thematic universe and its possibilities of change and to the nature of the information conveyed by these press forms.

The Print News Agenda During the War

The Schematic Nature of the News

The notion of the news is ambiguous, or at least manifests itself as a problematic concept. The written news media is a complex object in which highly different types of news simultaneously co-exist. Movie reviews, classified ads, auctions or sea and air traffic reports inhabit a textual and thematically heterogeneous universe that presents information we can call "practical". Practical information coexists with information about what we generally designate as being "current events". It is this latter concept that we commonly define as the *news*.

News can be defined as the particular discursive construction which narrates factual events generally ascribed to a possible world that is supposed to be the real world. This construction has a precise and identifiable graphic-thematic format, with a headline presenting the "topic" or principal argument to be developed, a group of subtitles that fulfil a summarising function, and a graphic mechanism that relates the different thematic units with an articulated pagination. The headlines and subtitles generally call on an encyclopaedic knowledge that the reader already possesses.

Generally, the news is integrated into a pagination format. This habituates the reader to recognise it at a glance by its graphic format and so to distinguish it from the movie schedule or the list of open drugstores. It thereby constructs a "mental model" in the reader that allows him or her visually and cognitively to distinguish a news item from other textual products. From a thematic point of view, these graphic-thematic units articulate themselves around a nucleus from which secondary or parallel topics can be extracted.

It seems apparent that it is not possible to assimilate "information" into the "news": the latter is the product of specific textual strategies. The information that circulates in the newsroom is greater than the number of news stories that end up appearing in the newspaper. For example, in a news item such as "Argentina reinforces its naval presence in the South Atlantic" (*Clarín,* 31 March), selected information is presented about the heightening of hostilities, diplomatic relations between Argentina and Great Britain, and the Argentine military junta's various cabinet meetings.

The elements that form the news story are hierarchically organised. They not only present a proper causal linearity, i.e. a temporality that mimes the temporality of the events, but always includes a certain type of embedding in the form of a summary, commentary or evaluation. From an enunciation viewpoint, this type of narration structures itself around a group of restrictions that are highly general and generalisable: there is no direct appeal to the reader, the narrator assumes an impersonal style, recourse is not made to colloquial language, but instead to a standard language from which personal and poetic traces are abolished. In this sense, the news story does not seek an aesthetic effect but aims toward a rapid understanding and precise interpretation on the part of the reader.

From the viewpoint of the Media Contract, the news story presents a dimension proper to the news discourse: the narrated events are generally both sufficiently assertive and evident that they can be accepted as truthful, or at least as non-fictitious, on the part of the reader.

In the media research tradition, the notion of "the news" is never separated from the concept of information flux, its appeal to different social sectors, and above all the notion of production that it implies. What are the criteria through which events are selected in order to become "news" in a newspaper? The relationship between the frequency of a particular event's occurrence and the *frequency* of its appearance in the newspaper is clearly a news production routine factor. Another *criteria* is the event's *clarity*: the less ambiguous the event is, the better its chance of being noticed and selected. *Relevance* indicates the site of the event's production (central nations versus peripheral ones). Finally, the criterion of *expectations* reveals that socio-cultural matrices exist from which the selection of a certain event "enters" into the circuit of expectations. This follows the known formula that the "news" is not precisely what we don't know – and is revealed to us by the press – but that in reality it is what people expect. The more events satisfy these criteria the better their chance of being selected as *newsworthy*.

The news produces an image of the world as "that which has really occurred" even though, as we have seen, elements subject to verification are not given. As such, in addition to the criteria in the process of selecting events that will become the news, a final criterion has also to be added: news *distortion*.[1]

Studying the different functions developed within a newspaper, Lester identifies the *gate-keeping* role assumed by the journalist, who

---

[1] Tuchman holds that the concept of "distortion" is foreign to the analysis of reality as a social construction. For him, "distortion" itself is socially constructed. Reality is constructed through a constant process of redefinition, reconsideration and revision.

must finally select the information that will enter the paper's agenda under the form of "the news". The journalist bases his or her decision on an inferential structure of selecting and interpreting that which is "newsworthy" and type-able (hard news, spot news, etc.) Lester demonstrates that news production is basically a routine and inter-organisational activity.

For Lester, the "news-object" is the result of increasingly framing the event. First, an organising frame provides a meaning-making device. Next, the event is framed by news' norms such as identification and classification. Finally, the story is framed by the angle or perspective under which it is presented (Lester 1980).

What links Lester's study to more recent works on the cognitive effects of a news story's structure is that framing stories are not a literal description of events, but, as we have already argued, an interpretation device, or, in the words of Lester, an interpretative device for actually assembling the essence of the occurrence.

Tuchman, another well known American sociologist, also highlights the news production activity as being inserted into a network that is not only social, but basically institutional. For this theorist, the "news" does not exist, just "news-events", in other words, the transformation and discursive accentuation of events made to conform to typification and classification critera. He argues that journalists write news-events according to how they happen and according to the demands of the newspaper's organisational structure (Tuchman 1978).

An hypothesis can be formulated that the news, like any discursive construction, operates by the simultaneous condensation and expansion of a basic narrative nucleus. To this process of macro-reducing impertinent details, a group of specificity conditions is added which include the identity and properties of the social actors involved, the use of cause and effect relationships, and the deictic functions of temporal or spatial signalling. In this way, a highly stable and repetitive schematic formula is constructed. As such, it is the way that a news story is presented (catastrophic titles, special reports, etc.) which profoundly marks its reception conditions

The reader is accustomed to the daily consumption of these highly structured textual forms in which the social world appears to be constructed in a routine way – in the sense of production routines – through a system of rapid causalities and identifications. These constructions presuppose a media fabric that permits it to be historically framed. It is the medium that, in its inter-dialogue with other medi,a establishes not only chronologies, but also the frequency of a news story's appearance – and disappearance – in public agendas.

In synthesis, the news establishes an actuality relevance and focus system through highlighting operations that go from headlines and titles to the frequency of an item's appearance. These operations submit the reader to a highly structured repetitive and routine reading code. This code permits the reader cognitively to organise his or her perception of the surrounding world with reference to that we commonly call "the news".[2]

The news is such a vacant form, a schemata of strongly standardised base rules, that the reader immediately assigns coherence to it because he or she recognises the discursive genre's type as clearly identifiable, pointing to a simple structure that does not differ from the pyramidal form well known to journalists, i.e. the classic "who, when, what, where and why" that fills the profession's training textbooks.

News about the Malvinas-Falklands

The "News about the Malvinas-Falklands" category is the construction of a textual object that is legitimised and selected from a newspaper's information flux in order to be studied as a mechanism made up of different dimensions.

Reviewing Argentine newspapers, one can find, for example, news items easily identifiable with the conflict, such as "The evolution of the controversy in the Southern Georgias is examined by the Military Junta", which appeared in *Clarín*'s political section on 30 March, or news items that touch on other themes but indirectly refer to the war and can thus enter into the same semantic universe. An example of this is "US veto in the UN", published in *Clarín*'s international section on 3 April. Reading this news item, the reader, after having passed through information concerning the American veto and a Security Council decision that had nothing to do with the Argentine situation, learns that the Security Council also had a closed door session about the conflict in the Malvinas-Falklands.

Finally, to further clarify this highly general definition of "News about the Malvinas-Falklands", we can refer to "practical information" such as the article about the "Book Convention" also published in *Clarín* on 3 April. The article alludes to the general public's interest in books about the Malvinas-Falklands. Subsequently, it is not possible to select only news items with titles specifically referring to the conflict.

---

[2] "Agenda-setting grows out of a general concern with how people organize and structure the world around them [...] the kind of cues which people attend to in structuring their world" (McCombs in Wilhoit 1981: 211).

Items that indirectly address the conflict must also be reviewed. It is precisely the alternation of these directly and indirectly Malvinas-Falklands concerned articles that allows us to detect the "news permeability syndrome" in the newspapers' strategies.

Highlighting the macro-semantic units that we call out of convenience "News about the Malvinas-Falklands" fractures the daily press's general universe and allows us to thematically sub-classify it so as to delineate the newspapers' agenda. In effect, the seeming heterogeneity of the press's thematic universe – the papers talk about everything – can be normalised through a specific qualitative criterion: what does the macro-semantic unit "News about the Malvinas-Falklands" report on and with what frequency?

It is possible to establish a group of subcategories that systematically repeat and contribute to the delineation of the press's agenda. For a diachronic analysis, these subcategories constitute an *a priori* reading criterion. For the moment, I will not work on the enunciation level. Instead, I will focus on content, i.e. on the level of what is being said. How these themes are being expressed, i.e. enunciation strategies, will be analysed in later chapters.

The presentation of certain issues in the press presupposes the centralisation and selection of a restricted number of contents which correspond to a "thematisation", i.e. the transformation and treatment of a certain number of distinctive events and facts in a single space of pertinence. The news sub-categories within the macro-semantic unit "News about the Malvinas-Falklands" are micro-narrations organised around a group of extremely stable and, as often happen with the news in general, repetitive themes. We can identify them as military, diplomatic, Argentine political, British political, economic, historical, religious, lifestyle, opinion, and other press issues. If we link these different news items together from a thematic viewpoint, we can observe the strongly stable formation of a group of thematic recurrences that develop, intensify, and repeat throughout the conflict. We can also identify the presence of clearly differentiated actors. We will see who are the actors and what scenes are in these news items.

Military news

Military news is made up of specific articles that narrated the war from a strictly military point of view. They were expressed through "communiqués" and "statements" made by exclusively, or allegedly exclusively, military press secretaries. Generally they included large accounts of troop movements, battle strategies, ship positions, etc. The vocabulary used was basically technical –it could hardly be otherwise.

As the conflict progressed, it developed true autonomy: the discourse became "expert" and the news items became increasingly more complex. Military news information sources were always institutional. In the last fifteen days of the conflict, military news dominated newspapers' agendas.

Political news
These items included political actions, statements and decisions made by the Military Junta, as well as the action of diverse national political figures. Political news items demarcated a scenario in which the military, politicians, business leaders and anyone who, at that moment, had become a character in the conflict, interacted. The traditional political class manifested, with some reservations, a certain support for the war. Through the Multipardiaria group, a type of extra-official opinion organisation that nucleused political parties outlawed by the Military Junta, they won a large space of democratic negotiation. The imminent end of the war found politicians in direct opposition to the war and the Military Junta. This was evident in the statements of ex-president Arturo Frondizi and the then Radical politician Raúl Alfonsín when each learned of the Argentine defeat. Each, though, maintained a cautious attitude and conscientiously measured the role he might play in the post-war future.

Diplomatic news
Like military news, diplomatic news was also specific and circumscribed to the closed universe of the Argentine diplomatic world, i.e. the Argentine Ministry of Foreign Affairs and the United Nations. These news items took the form of statements, interviews, and quotations. They maintained a large amount of autonomy when compared to military and political news.

> "Our information sources were in the Office of Foreign Relations. We also had information from our embassies. There were no press secretaries in Foreign Relations and the only person who transmitted information was the Minister himself, Costa Méndez." (Interview with Ambassador Atilio Molteni, then Minister in the Argentine Embassy in London during the war, Buenos Aires, 20 December 1990).

British News About the Conflict
These news items narrated the conflict according to the British perspective. Their protagonists pertained to the British political world

with its lobbies, interests and debates. When the conflict began, these articles were included within the Argentine diplomatic news section, but as the situation moved toward a complete rupture of diplomatic relations, they increased in independence until becoming a pole of autonomous power within the Argentine institutional interplay. These reports were also the site of threats, challenges, and the "no comments" of the British government.

News about American politics

Dedicated to narrating the American government interventions and negotiations, from interviews with President Ronald Reagan to those with Secretary of State Alexander Haig, these news pieces gave information about the American position throughout the war. As the conflict worsened, news reports about American politics were differentiated from those about Britain, but they did not manage to attain the autonomy of the latter. The articles attained a high amount of agenda coverage and importance in the month of May when the United States finally aligned itself with Great Britain. In the last week of the conflict, contradictions in American foreign policy became obvious with its changing votes in the United Nations.

Economic news

These news stories dealt with the European Community's sanctions against the Argentine economy during the conflict. The papers were filled with Argentine press secretaries and business leaders supporting the conflict who became virtual wandering ambassadors attempting to gain support for Argentina's position in international fora. Secondary in respect to political and diplomatic news, economic news maintained a relative level of autonomy thanks to its technical vocabulary.

Historical news

This type of news item was principally published in the first few weeks of the conflict so as to remind readers about the history of the islands and the dispute with Great Britain over their possession. They appeared regularly in magazines and weekly news magazines throughout the entire war. Historical news took charge of presenting highly synthesised chronological narrations of the conflict's antecedents and causes. This group of items constituted one of the argumentative registers in the press's discourse.

Lifestyle news

Lifestyle news erupted in the first week of the conflict to offer readers picturesque narrations showing the war's immediate and everyday aspects. It constituted half of the information presented in weekly news magazines. "How do kelpers live and what do they do?", "What our soldiers are doing today", and "A typical day for our boys in the Malvinas" were the most presented themes. With a zoom lens effect, these news stories managed to bring images of a far-away war closer to a reader who had never set foot in the islands. The articles were generic and autonomous and their character, contrary to the antecedent categories, were anonymous and pertained to the private sector. Lifestyle news was almost exclusively articulated in a narrative register.

Religious news
Religious news dealt with the Catholic Church's institutional universe and the responses of other religious denominations to the war. Present throughout the conflict, they acquired a fundamental importance in the war's final three weeks, with Pope John Paul II's trip to Argentina and the Argentine bishops' call for peace at any price in order to avert tragedy. These articles took the form of narrations, statements and documents. Like military and diplomatic news, their sources were also institutional.

Opinion news
Generally constructed from signed articles or editorials, these items represented the argumentative register and described cause-effect relationships in the conflict. While being hierarchical, they were also interpretative of the history that they narrated. Opinions were tangential to the news discourse and formed part of the press's internal sources. Only present at the beginning and end of the war, opinion items had the role of focusing on some of the conflict's elements.

News based on other media
Irregular, but increasingly present as the war progressed, these news articles published the opinions and reactions of the British press and dealt with problems of censorship, counter-information and rumours. News based on other media formed a veritable micro-account in the discourse and represented the Argentine viewpoint about the international press. This type of item was basically made up of the British press and figures from the world of journalism. These articles never dealt with the functioning of the Argentine press except to differentiate it from the British one. The issue of censorship or self-censorship in the Argentine press was never addressed.

A Quantitative Reading

This thematic classification can be seen as complementary to the classic classifications made by other researchers about the field of journalism. In effect, it is journalists themselves who provide the internal classification of the events chosen for their articles on the basis of that which is considered to be potentially interesting material. This classification, which is particularly valid for the American press industry, becomes pertinent in the case of the Malvinas-Falklands conflict because it includes five news "types" differentiated by their contents and subjects. The five types are Hard News, Soft News, Continuing News, Spot News and Developing News.

Clearly, this type of classification is highly practical and can be related to the type of daily tasks that the journalist must fulfil under concrete and precise standardised criteria in the productive organisation that is the newspaper. Performing a quantitative classification, in other words, a classification based on the frequency and amount of information expressed in "News about the Malvinas-Falklands" during the entire conflict by the two main Argentine newspapers, demonstrates:

	La Nación	*Clarín*
Total news items from 2 April 1982 to 16 June 1982	7325	8510
Malvinas- Falklands news items	2161	4529
% of Malvinas-Falklands news items	29.5%	53.2%
Mean number of total news items per day	99	115
Mean number of Malvinas-Falklands news items	29	61

Table 6

Aside from being eloquent, these figures indicate the Argentine press's effort literally to "cover" the event in an exhaustive manner despite the restrictions they were under in terms of information sources and military censorship. The data indicates that a third of all information published by *La Nación* and more than half published by *Clarín* made reference to the war. In the weekly news magazines analysed, no differences were found, and the information universe of "News about the Malvinas-Falklands" made up 90% of the material published.

This profusion of information spanning first to last page of newspapers and magazines confirms, at least from a quantitative viewpoint, the presence of the "news permeability syndrome" in the newspapers and the "Malvinisation of information syndrome" in weekly news magazines. It also raises a question: just who or what were the information sources within this considerable information flux?

The Strategic Use of Sources During the War
A quantitative analysis of the frequency with which "News about the Malvinas-Falklands" appeared in the two newspapers analysed supports the initial hypothesis: the Argentine written press system suffered from a "news Malvinisation syndrome". In other words, the Argentine written press was monopolised by, and focused on, one event: the war with Great Britain. It is now indispensable to study the information sources that *La Nación* and *Clarín* used to produce these news stories. In short, who were the principal Argentine newspapers' sources and what function did they carry out?

In a classic study on American news production rituals, Herbert Gans (1979: 116-145) holds that the systematic use of information sources reflects "the hierarchy of the state and the society". The Argentine press generally used a reduced quantity of information sources selected according to an essentially practical criterion: how efficient were they?

A source is used when it lends weight to the news story and offers a high level of productivity – for example, when it provokes. A source is also used when it occupies an important position in the political, economic or social structure, when the information that this source gives out is credible, trustworthy, and does not require the journalist to verify it later. Finally, sources are used on the basis of their geographic proximity to both the narrated events and, above all, to the journalist. This last characteristic, the source's close proximity to the journalist, is what is known as "local sources".

These relevant characteristics determine the four criteria that predominated in the Argentine newspapers' selection of information sources: level of authority in the general power structure; the productivity of the information given; its credibility and trustworthiness; and finally the source's proximity to the theatre of operations or simply to the powerful. It is not by chance that in Argentina the most used source has always been "an official" one.

Another element to keep in mind for a study of Argentine sources' functioning is that, even if the source itself doesn't determine the news story's value, this value implicitly appears in the information that the source gives. It seems that the process of assigning value or "enhancing" is inherent to Argentine sources' basic functioning.

Gans's classification indicates that the most used information sources in American newspapers are "another newspaper" or "another journalist". This finding reinforces the media's credibility effect and, above all, its coherence as a permanent system of feedback loops. In the case of Argentina, the principal information source after the official one is another newspaper's journalist. Gans's study is useful here in its reference to information from military or ecclesiastical sources, institutions defined by Erwin Goffman as "total" because they possess enough *esprit de corps* to inhibit their members from speaking independently to the press. Obviously, in the case of the military, reticence about giving official information is motivated, as Gans notes, by the fact that no news is published during war-time that can compromise the bellicose power (1979: 188).

Another study of Italian origin on sources' functioning (Cesareo 1981: 72) confirms Gans's hypothesis about sources' situation on a power pyramid. This study analyses the "faith and symbolic" relationship that is installed between sources and journalists. Sources should be stable and central – parallel to political stability – territorial and event-oriented. Cesareo classifies "active sources" as those which offer information of their own initiative and "passive sources" as those which the journalist must seek out. Analysing the use of Argentine information sources, active sources (in other words, those that directly lend themselves to giving information) are rarely used, while passive sources occupy only third place. This implies that a large amount of re-elaboration and seeking of information occurs on the part of reputable journalists. What is interesting about the source-journalist relationship, be it passive or active, is, as Cesareo notes, the sense that those elements of reality which do not enter into the source-circuit tend to be cancelled out (1981: 72).

A third study, also of Italian origin (Lepri 1982: 30-45), can be applied to the Argentine case. This study shows the differences between newspapers' own sources and the use of governmental and international press agencies. The latter are defined in terms of a veritable service industry: they are organisations whose business is to pick up, develop and sell news items like an industrial product. In Latin America, Agence France Press (AFP) is the most used international press agency source, followed by American United Press International (UPI) and United Press (UP).

Once again, the Argentine case has its own characteristics. *Clarín* followed the norm of using the Latin American predominant AFP – at least during the analysed period – as its main source, while *La Nación* used the American Associated Press (AP). What is particularly noteworthy, however, is that both newspapers almost completely set aside the use of Argentine governmental press agencies, such as TELAM. Differences such as these in the use of information sources are important, given that Lepri considers the differentiating element in a newspaper's information strategy to be the way in which information sources are used. Lepri goes further – and thus helps to explain the lack of use of the TELAM agency – in affirming the presupposition of the objectivity news aspires to, in its attempt to offer quality information, "sticking to the facts", also known as the "factuality" of British newspapers. Factuality is supposed to guarantee the objectivity that determines the use of an agency as an information source.

An article synthesising American studies, such as that by Tuchman, signals that established and well known information networks institutionalise the use of particular information sources and ignore others. As such, the news net imposes order in the social world, making the news event always occur in one area of the planet and not in another (Tuchman 1978: 38ff.). From this postulate, the large relevance of information from central countries as opposed to that of peripheral nations can be derived. The Malvinas-Falklands war, and later the Gulf war, are cases in which information from a peripheral nation erupted in and occupied central nations' information map, thereby inverting the tendency noted by Tuchman. This eruption was possible – just as it was in Baghdad – because the conflict's interlocutor was always a central nation.

In terms of agency information's homogeneity noted in van Dijk's (1987) study, which analysed international news in 250 newspapers of peripheral nations, it turns out that about half (49%) of the information that circulates in these countries uses "other news media" as the their sources. In this way, two fundamental characteristics of the source system are delineated: the auto-legitimisation of the press system as a principal information source, i.e. the legitimisation and guarantee that we have already referred to, and the homogenisation of public events that includes an "echo" effect. In the case of van Dijk's analysis, what follows other news media as sources are political-institutional ones. The latter are useful sources because of their proximity to those in power and their societal position.

Italian researcher Agostini (1984) notes that the use of sources "reinforces power relationships". The higher one is on the social ladder, the easier the relationship with press becomes, determining in this way the politics-press relationship. Consequently, the lower one is on the social ladder, the farther one is from becoming a potential information source. The corollary to this observation is that some do not have access to the media world since there is a reciprocally conditioned and highly exclusive interaction relationship between sources and the media. The Argentine case does not exactly follow the same hierarchical tendency. In our analysis of the themes included in the "News about the Malvinas-Falklands" category, we were able to show that not only the Argentine newspapers, but also all its weekly news magazines, gave a large amount of space to autonomous speech, to the "average citizen" source, in other words, to the construction of an everyday social actor elevated to the category of public figure. A possible interpretative hypothesis about this phenomenon is that an information source that represented the "average Argentine" in newspapers and news magazines was used to help society identify with the war's anonymous soldiers and actors.

Finally, a study by Miguel Rodrigo Alsina (1989: 135-8) presents contextualisation as a specific journalistic activity. According to Rodrigo Alsina, newspapers pre-structure an event, thereby imbuing it with a new value so that it can quickly be contextualised. We have already seen how historical news in "news about the Malvinas-Falklands" category basically carried out this function at the conflict's beginning. In terms of information sources' functioning, the source becomes the focus the journalist calls on to concretise his or her competency and "frame" the event.

In this way, it is possible to trace an itinerary that moves from total dependence between source and journalist to cooperation and interchange of the same objects, as in the case of diffusing information *versus* keeping it. In this case, it is the source that simultaneously makes the news, as did Argentina's military communiqués during the war. What is prevalent in Alsina's study is that sources are institutionalised by virtue of the fact that a group of social actors has simultaneous access to the halls of power and the press.

INFORMATION SOURCES AND NEWS PRODUCTION

It seems evident that the issue of the use of information sources during a war is a recurrent problem in the study of news production routines. It forms part of the debate about the objectivity of information that comes from sources. I will not fully treat this complex problem until I present concrete analyses in Part Two of this book, in which I will attempt to demonstrate that objectivity is a meaning effect produced by a particular textual strategy accomplished by the simultaneous manipulation of information sources and the construction of narrative worlds. It is important, however, to present some criteria and viewpoints in order to address the criterion of "objectivity", at least as this concept has been analysed in the American and European sociological traditions.

Perhaps it has been American researcher Guy Tuchman who has most developed the criterion of journalistic objectivity. In his article "Objectivity as a strategic ritual" (1972), Tuchman holds that journalism is permanently confronted with the need for immediate decision-making in order to validate the attention and credibility of the material it presents on a daily basis, with which it produces (Tuchman 1980, 186). This decision-making process can be organised into four strategies for verifying the narrated objectivity: a) using sources with different view-points about the event; b) presenting evidence that consists in individualising supplementary information that is normally accepted as being credible; c) using quotes that permit citing seemingly undistorted opinions and annulling the journalist's direct intervention; and d) structuring the information in a sequential order.

For Tuchman, the notions of objectivity and objective are tied to a veritable ritual of elaborating social reality's events. The concept of *objectivity* can be defined as concentrating on objects external to the mind while *objective* can be defined as pertaining more to the object of thought than to the thinking subject. From a philosophical viewpoint, these two definitions oppose objective and subjective within a theory of knowledge and reality-apprehension. They are completed with the notion of "common sense", which plays a fundamental role in the evaluation of contents. For Tuchman, common sense allows one to determine if a particular news story contains all the necessary conditions that allow one to accept it as fact. For its part, "common sense" tangentially addresses the criterion of social pre-construction, despite their diverse origins: "pre-construction" is knowledge shared and accepted by the linguistic community about a particular discursive wisdom, while common reality is a sociological concept that indicates social agreement forms about everyday reality.

During the 1980s, the Vietnam War became the primary theatre of debate about the American press's objectivity, as it is today the Iraq war. Changes in values, evaluation and objectivity criteria in news presentation, especially through the selection of stories published at the beginning of the war, allowed consideration of this war's narration by the American media as a case study that established jurisprudence in the treatment of war information.

In a well known book by British authors Morrison and Tumber (1988) about war correspondents on the front lines, the Vietnam war initially appeared in the American media as a conflict between the United States and its allies against communism. Morrison and Tumber argue that standard values changed as of the Tet offensive in 1968. The offensive signalled an end to doubts about both the need for involvement in the war and the honesty of the US government when reporting to the press. The press initially described the conflict in Vietnam as a civil war, thus calling to mind the American Civil War. The press quickly realised the Civil War was based on standard values shared by all. Perception of the Vietnam conflict then changed to one in which it was seen as an episode in the Cold War. Once American troops arrived on the Vietnamese front, the conflict was placed under US domestic news and no longer under foreign news (Morrison and Tumber 1988: 200-203).

Analysing the function of television during a war situation and television's influence on the American public, the authors studied the complex information and counter-information web in which the American press became involved. During the Vietnam War, television was accused of over-using tapes of actual battles and patrols. Journalists privately admitted that doing this was questionable, but that they could not change the way the war was covered. Journalists justified their collaboration with the government and the military by noting that this was the first war in which the press was not under the control of official censors. The CIA was paying journalists to spread their reports about the Vietcong and the FBI infiltrated journalists into peaceful demonstrations. Horrible stories were being circulated that were unlikely to be believed by the mass public, like the My Lai massacre, and the ear-trophies cut off Vietcong prisoners (270-5).

The interplay between common sense and the construction of a veridiction effect, taken together with the sense of institutional pressure to cover the war appropriately, is one thing the Vietnamese conflict has in common with the Falklands-Malvinas war, despite differences in the two conflicts' durations.

Information Sources and News Production

In a series of qualitative interviews that I conducted with 24- to 50-year old Argentines about the press's credibility and consumption during the war, the suspicion of having been presented "distorted information" is strong and current:

"It was drivel given by Galtieri. They falsified information, they were liars. But Argentina is generally like that. The press is like that, there isn't a culture of criticising, or of informing. The media has total impunity." (Jorge J., 46, businessman).

"I believed them (the press) all equally. I didn't believe one more than another. I also didn't trust any of them because deep down I knew that they were lying to us, but it was a lie and illusion I wanted to believe. The media illusion. I knew that playing with information was part of war. [...] In any case, I enjoyed all the Argentine exploits. But I think that it was false information. In terms of the result: up until two days before the beating; we were going to win and later they had to admit that we'd lost!" (Norberto V., 37, architect)

"You had to see that the press was controlled by the government like the television, that they falsified information. The written press tried to adjust its search for the truth. The magazines in general were orientated to sensationalism and didn't have much to do with news. In general, the media based itself on official information sources that were very popular, but weren't objective about the conflict. I believed in *Clarín*'s political analysis and in that paper's foreign information sources." (Raúl R., 35, businessman).

"I had good information because I had friends in the military. I never trusted the press, because they steer and distort the news. An example? The Navy's decisions. The internal power struggles in the military were very complex and there wasn't ever any real access to what was actually happening in the upper ranks." (Francisco O., 35, union leader).

"In the end, no one dared to say that we'd lost." (Nestor A., 24, student).

Empirical and Textual Sources

Returning to the use of information sources and its relation to journalistic objectivity during the war, it is surprising that all of the earlier studies cited (which are all useful for delineating different classifications of the used information sources' categories) make no reference to an essential theoretical distinction between empirical sources and textual ones, as well as the fact that the source always presents itself as a discursive construction. In effect, the cited studies consider sources from an empirical perspective, as if no mediation or transformation existed between the source and the production of the news story. By confusing the textual strategies presented by the newspaper, these studies participate in the same illusion proposed by the media contract. The press genre has the power to make some social actors acquire the status of "public figures" instead of just historical figures, thanks to his or her construction as a direct or indirect information source.

When working with information texts, i.e. with the textual fragments that we call "the news", the first thing that jumps to the eye is that almost the entire represented universe is introduced into the newspaper through a specific index: reference to the information source. The entire narrated event is re-structured from the start by a progressive framing which generates different textual movements such as identifying or obscuring the public figure in play. It is precisely this reconstruction that contributes to the generation of not only the credibility effect on which the written press bases itself, but also two of the newspaper genre's favourite ploys: rebuttals and "rumours". In this way, the information source becomes a textual function.

One of the newspaper's first operations is to organise narrations that have sources as their principal figures, i.e. those that literally "report". The newspaper assigns them a fact-finding mission and specific actions to be carried out: what is being said in the diplomatic, military, political worlds, etc. The structure of sources that the press presupposes becomes the simulacrum of social hierarchy, and above all, the emitter's system's structure. This crucial function developed for sources in the news story's textual structure by newspapers categorically signals one of the genre's fundamental characteristics: the construction of a referential space perceived by the reader as being both current (the sources are on-scene and "speak") and highly real (the events must have occurred this way because the sources' accounts legitimise the report). As such, the written press becomes similar to television.

If, as the reviewed authors have noted, the interaction between an empirical source and a journalist is determinant in news production, then the inter-relation between a textual source and public opinion about the event addressed by the discourse is just as important. We can predict that every source produces an image of public opinion, a twofold movement in which the media proposes both a contextual, informative reading pact to, and establishes a gradation of credibility with, its readers. This occurs thanks to a certain internal legitimacy lag between references to "official sources" and the use of extra-official newspaper sources. The lag intervenes between information whose origin can be precisely identified and that which cannot.

The explicit presence of sources in Argentine newspapers was constructed as a way to legitimise the information. The sources' different interactions determined the theatre of enunciative operations carried out on the newspapers. In effect, who "spoke" during the conflict? And above all, which information sources did the newspapers use?

Newspapers' Own Sources
The sources used during the sixty-four days of the conflict by *La Nación* and *Clarín* can be divided into two main categories: the newspaper's own sources and international and national agency sources. These sources were composed of the ensemble of journalists, reporters, editors, and correspondents who covered the war. By making reference to their own journalistic experience, either by signing reports or using the by-lines "*Clarín* was there" or "According to a *La Nación* reporter", they established a radial extension that managed to constitute over half of the newspapers' information. Even if statistical indices reveals that most of the information expressed through the written press uses national and international agency sources, Argentina's *Clarín* and *La Nación* inverted this tendency during the war:

	La Nación	Clarín
% internal sources	70.68%	57.08%

Table 7

The journalistic task of being an internal source necessitated a presence in the principal centres of political decision-making such as the Presidential Palace, the Ministry of Foreign Affairs, diverse military offices, naval and aeronautic bases in the country's south, and, of course, major American and European capitals. *La Nación* and *Clarín* had correspondents in London, Washington and New York, itinerant reporters in Paris, Madrid, and Havana, and special envoys in the Malvinas-Falklands. Because of the upcoming British invasion, all Argentine journalists had to leave the islands in April by order of the Military Junta. The use of internal sources in *La Nación* and *Clarín* can be explained by the fluidity of their contact with the governing classes. A cover-up by these papers is indicated through their use of stable information sources in diverse political lobbies, which found resonance in both newspapers. Seen from this viewpoint, the two newspapers do not escape Tuchman and Gans's characterisation of the relationship between sources and the power pyramid.

In the face of the rising world tendency to use the large information monopolies that agencies are, *La Nación*'s and *Clarín*'s tendency to use internal sources could also indicate a particular conceptualisation of the press tied to the deontology of the press a hundred years ago. Furthermore, *La Nación*'s doubling of its use of internal sources reveals a system of capillary penetration highly rooted in Argentina's traditional ruling class, while *Clarín* signals its proximity to modern journalistic practices through its use of press agencies.

Interviewed about the way in which *Clarín* used information sources, Ricardo Kirschbaum, *Clarín* editor during the conflict who, with Oscar Raúl Cardoso and Eduardo van der Kooy, co-authored one of the most authoritative books on the Malvinas-Falklands war, affirmed:

> "You had to decide between either military information or agency cables. There was no other alternative. It was a war in which there was no independent press, just an official one. *Clarín*, for example, didn't have journalists stationed on the islands, neither did any other Argentine media. The TELAM agency, though, was there throughout the whole war." (Interview with journalist Ricardo Kirschbaum, editor in chief of *Clarín*, Buenos Aires, 17 December 1990).

In an interview written by Bartolomé Mitre, director and owner of *La Nación*, Mitre lists the information sources used by his newspaper. His statements coincide with those of Kirschbaum about the legitimacy of the Argentine Ministry of Foreign Affairs' information sources:

> "*La Nación*'s sources were the Argentine Chancery, the Armed Forces, political parties, Argentine specialists on foreign politics, and, naturally, members of the Executive wing. Added to these national sources were national and international diplomatic ones,

United Nations and Organization of American States officials, foreign newspaper correspondents, etc. In Argentina, our information was received by war reporters from *La Nación*, covering official, private, and diplomatic organisations. Outside of Argentina, the information came through our correspondents in Europe and the Americas, as well as those covering international organisations. Foreign news cables were always used, including those that came from Great Britain." (Written response by Dr Bartolomé Mitre, former director of *La Nación*, Buenos Aires, 17 December 1990).

Beyond the difficulties that the Argentine press experienced in covering the information and "how" it narrated the war, there is a point that rises from the figures about the use of information sources in the so-called "serious" press. The considerable prominence of internal sources over agency ones in both of the analysed newspapers undoubtedly constitutes not only an attempt to construct an "opinion" press during the war that was independent from the great centres of world news production but, above all, an attempt to differentiate itself from military source information. This tendency is accentuated if we keep in mind the small percentage of government agency material used.

National and international agency sources
DYN and TELAM were Argentina's national and governmental news agencies. They made up an extremely low percentage of the sources used and cited by both *La Nación* and *Clarín*. This percentage never went beyond 3% of all the information presented in these papers. It is possible that the papers considered DYN's and TELAM's information to be superfluous and biased as opposed to the information received from international agencies. Whatever were the reasons that led *La Nación* and *Clarín* not to use information from Argentina's national news agencies, this action reveals at the very least these agencies' weak capacity for interpretation and adaptation to the construction of the newspapers' agendas.

According to *La Nación*, international agency information and reports about the war were provided by 200 foreign journalists: 46 from the United States, 54 from Great Britain, 12 from Brazil, 10 from Canada, 9 from Spain, 8 each from Chile and Japan, 6 each from France and West Germany, 4 each from Mexico, Norway, Peru and Uruguay, and 1 each from Ireland, Holland, Austria, Saudi Arabia, Venezuela, Denmark, and Switzerland (source: *La Nación*, 10 April). These sources made up an important percentage of those used by the two Argentine newspapers being examined.

	La Nación	*Clarín*
% use Agency information	25.3%	42.88%
AFP (France)	3.6%	7.66%
EFE (Spain)	3.7%	7.35%
ANSA (Italy)	5.4%	7.17%
AP (USA)	6.4%	6.53%
UPI (USA)	4.7%	5.54%
Latin Reuters (U.K)	1.8%	5.21%
TELAM (Argentina's official agency)	1.6%	0.97%

Table 8

Official Information: the Argentine Military Government

From the first week of the conflict, the Military Junta expressly prohibited access to the islands by journalists. Nevertheless, there were a restricted number of Argentine journalists stationed on the islands with military authorisation. These journalists supplied material to weekly news magazines. Later on, those journalists working in Argentina's southern naval bases were obliged to leave these observation stations (*Clarín*, 8 April, "Statements by the Minister of Interior, General Saint Jean").

In terms of the military's control of the press during the conflict, it can be argued that initially the Military Junta's government sought to achieve a "participatory" position with the country's principal newspapers in order to construct a favourable public opinion of the conflict, at least during its first weeks. Only two examples of this tendency can be cited for the month of April: a meeting between Public Press Secretary, Rodolfo Baltiérrez, and the directors of the Buenos Aires newspapers to inform them of the events that culminated in the Argentine landing on the Malvinas-Falklands (*Clarín*, 3 April, "The press is informed"; *La Nación*, 3 April, "Newspaper directors in the Casa Rosada"); and the centralisation of information in the Armed Forces Headquarters:

> Yesterday morning, journalists stationed in the naval zone of Bahia Blanca were informed that, from now on, all news about the conflict with Great Britain would be centralised in the Buenos Aires' Armed Forces Headquarters. Questioned about this act and

the "military silencing" that the resolution implies, military spokesmen explained that it was a "useful and efficient" resolution meant to meet the needs of both the international and national press. (*Clarín*, 14 April, "The air bridge with the islands is confirmed, some submarines have been detected").

With the worsening of the conflict towards the end of April, the unfruitful negotiations performed by the American Secretary of State Alexander Haig and the re-conquering of the Georgia Islands by the British, the Armed Forces had total control of all information about the war. The resolution was published in its totality on the first page of *La Nación*'s 30 April edition:

> *Decree by which the Military Junta takes control of the press for reasons of national security*
> Given the situation with the United Kingdom, the Military Junta declares:
> Article 1. – All information and news coming from outside of the country, whatever their origin, used by the press, and all information diffused by the written, oral, or televised press that is any way related to military operations and national security is subject to the control of the Armed Forces.
> Article 2. – The Armed Forces exercises control of information conveyed by all of the press under its power.
> Article 3. – The directors and editors of the different news media will be considered personally responsible for all transgressions against Article 1.
> Article 4. – All transgressions will be sanctioned with the immediate closure of the news media in question and with the arrest of the responsible director or editor for an undetermined amount of time.

Despite the severe tone of the text, none of Argentina's principal newspapers were closed down during the war. As was to be revealed later though, they did suffer from a news blackout during the conflict final weeks. Journalist Oscar Raúl Cardoso, interviewed for this study, told of the practices of *Clarín* journalists and his perception of the era's censorship and auto-censorship:

> I covered all the information coming from the United States. I particularly remember being in New York. Iit was a key moment in the negotiations. I went back to my hotel, turned on the television

and saw CBS news, The first thing they showed was some BBC footage. I called Buenos Aires. The editor's office answered and they euphorically said, "We have sunk the *Invincible*." I was seeing something else, live, at that moment on the television screen. I said to them, "Look, I'm seeing something to the contrary," and they answered, "That's all just a psychological ploy."

I used to eat dinner with British journalists. They also distorted. I was with the journalistic director of the BBC during his conflict with Mrs Thatcher when he affirmed, "The BBC doesn't need Mrs Thatcher to give it lessons in patriotism." This type of attitude was absent in Argentina at the time. In the research we did for the book, we saw that the news expressed two clear objectives: a) gestating military thinking about the war; for example, the fact that the United States was supporting us and that Russia was going to help us by intervening, and b) when this turned out to be impossible, we had to deny the facts. What the military government did wasn't so much to sustain a lie as to prevent the rest of the world's reports about the war penetrating into Argentina. This was already clear with the issue of the disappeared. The response was, "I didn't know anything about it." There was also the complicity of the public: the public wanted to believe that they didn't know anything.

I arrived in Buenos Aires from New York two days before the defeat and I remember that there was no awareness of what was happening; people still thought we were winning. The press was clearly responsible for the construction of this image: the press lied by omission more than by action. It abandoned its role as a watchdog; when we were at war, the press didn't question. And when reality didn't fit, it was censored. It was an internal self-censorship. (Interview with journalist Oscar Raúl Cardoso, from *Clarín*, Buenos Aires, 17 December 1990)

The case of British press censorship was completely different. It is well known that the control of political news in Britain is a tradition established by *ad hoc* legislation dating from the 1800s. An open political press control system had always existed and this can be understood by the functioning of the British press, which is entirely different from that of its European colleagues. The British press functions under the Lobby system. This system was created in 1884 to regulate relations between the press and the government. It allowed the presence of a small number of correspondents in Parliament, approximately 140 political journalists at the time of the war. These journalists are the only ones authorised to cover government information and to have access to political documents without having to reveal their sources. As of 1912, the D News (Defence news) system has also functioned. Under this system, news concerning defence issues is submitted to the Minister of Defence. Editors and journalists can publish information in this area only with the express authorisation of the Minister. The D News office is made up of members of the Ministry of Defence, Ministry of Foreign Affairs, and selected members of the British press.

This generalised legal control system has allowed the development of a counter-system of information leaks, confidential information, scandals and revelations that have historically nourished the functioning of the British press, at least in its reference to public figures, such as stories dealing with the private lives of government ministers, but it has never, properly speaking, transgressed the line drawn around military information (Hooper 1982; Neguine 1989). A 1985 study performed by the Glasgow University Media Group notes: "Of all these formal constraints, the Official Secrets Acts is potentially the most wide ranging, since it means in effect that all government information is secret unless an 'official' statement is made about it. [...] There is now a large number of documented cases of programmes being censored, delayed or banned" (1985: 3, 4). The Malvinas-Falklands war represented an important moment in Britain's history of military information control. The Glasgow University Media Group further argues that: "The restriction on what could be reported fell into three broad areas: (1) the limits imposed directly by the Ministry of Defence in the form of censorship and controls on journalists; (2) the restraints of the 'normal' system of lobby briefings ; and (3) controls which broadcasters imposed upon themselves in the name of 'taste' or in reference to what they saw as 'public opinion'" (1985: 8).

These interactive systems between censorship and auto-censorship were described during the war by *The Economist* as being either "voluntary censorship", applied to all journalists in general from the application of "D News"; "compulsory censorship" applied to journalists stationed in the British naval force ; and "grey censorship", which was the censorship exercised by the Naval hierarchy among the different ships that made up the Task Force.

The Media as Sources
In summary, textual sources are the enunciation pact that the newspaper establishes with its readers to present social actors as informants. Textual sources cross the totality of empirical sources and acquire a major level of personalisation and legitimacy. Classifying these sources lets us establish at least four categories:

First place is held by the overall press, television, radio, and the newspapers, that is itself considered as information macro-actants. It developed different narrative programmes (discovering, informing, confirming, etc.) that generally covered the modality of "knowing". It was highly stable and appeared in news items about the news itself as well as in almost all the news that referred to the war. Its level of legitimacy was extremely high because it supported itself on the entire credibility of the press.

In second place we find official institutional textual sources. These include the entire universe of informants whose names can be cited (presidents, cabinet ministers, diplomats, politicians, etc.) Their principal characteristic was that they could be easily identified as members of political or social institutions.

Thirdly, the notion of unofficial sources designates those social actors whose identification is imprecise, whether it be because they want to maintain anonymity, or because the information that they transmit can give rise to rumours since it is not easily verifiable. Unofficial textual sources constitute the so-called "off the record" information. They can be divided as active or passive unofficial textual sources on the basis of the personalisation or depersonalisation that they present.

Finally, active unofficial sources present an acceptable level of identification that lets them be inscribed into a specific referential universe, such as "the military", "politicians", or "diplomats". They are represented by phrases such as "military sources in London" or "well informed sources from the Central Bank", etc. They generally give information that different lobbies are interested in transmitting. For this reason, they are called "active".

Counter to this, passive unofficial sources are impersonal because they do not offer explicit statements about their origin. They are represented by expressions such as "observers maintain that" or "some state that". This characterisation of passive unofficial sources signals a two-fold enunciative movement that is present in the way that the newspaper gives information. On the one hand, they actualise the modality of "having to": the newspaper should pick up all the versions of a story, even those that it cannot confirm. On the other hand, these sources let newspapers publish that which has the dimension of being "secret" as an information modality.

In effect, the strategy of giving secret information does not exclusively originate in the need to hide or deny/suppress information. This type of strategy is not related to the existence, or lack of existence, of censorship or auto-censorship. Instead, it is closely tied to the enunciation forms through which a determined piece of information wants to be transmitted.

The manipulation of secret information allows the newspaper to: a) decide if the event can be transformed into a news story; b) make verification of the published information and its source difficult or impossible; c) accredit the event as being authentic; d) enhance the information in such a way that its status of being secret transforms it into a "revelation"; and e) produce events that are "adapted" to a particular circumstance or an opportune moment in time. For this reason, the imprecision or depersonalisation of sources offers a high amount of freedom in deciding which events are newsworthy. The recourse to these textual sources makes verifying the information given highly difficult, but at the same time casts dates, places, and persons on the press scene with the objective of making them circulate.

We will now consider the percentage of use of different sources in the analysed newspapers.

	La Nación	*Clarín*
Other media sources	25.72%	19.09%
Institutional/official sources	24.24%	13.84%
Passive unofficial sources	17.12%	18.94%
Active unofficial sources	3.6%	5.21%

Table 9

Despite the fact that *Clarín* prioritised, though minimally, other media as sources, this newspaper generally used all textual sources in a completely homogenous manner. *Clarín* seems to have been equitable in the space it gave to different enunciators: other media forms spoke, but so did official sources, and there was space for unverified information and rumours. *La Nación*, however, preferred to use institutional sources and maintained a strategy of strongly legitimising the newspaper's word. In effect, as I shall demonstrate in the following pages, *Clarín* was the more permeable of the two as far as the use of rumours was concerned.

"What do all these rumours mean?"

Among the interpretative hypotheses that can be formulated about the unleashing of the Argentine-British war with the landing of Argentine troops on 2 April, the one that appears to be the most exhaustive and probable is the one that cites the close relationship between the economic crisis and the political institution. According to this hypothesis, the Argentine Military Junta and the government decided to find a subject that would galvanise public opinion so as to shed itself of internal pressures. This subject was Argentina's claim to sovereignty over the Malvinas-Falklands (Hastings and Jenkins 1983; Cardoso *et al.* 1983; Verbitsky 1984).

The effect produced by the Argentine landing, on not only the British and Argentine but the entire international press, was a surprise. The Argentine newspapers registered the political-diplomatic escalation that would culminate in the Military government's decision to recuperate the islands through military action, but this did not achieve the "surprise" effect expressed by the press in general. In the days that immediately preceded the landing, the press agenda was dedicated to the general strike of 31 March organised by the General Labour Confederation (Confederación General del Trabajo, CGT). This was the first labour strike organised after the 1976 military takeover, which overthrew the democratic government of General Juan Domingo Perón's widow and initiated a new period of bloodshed in Argentine political history with its high level of assassinations and disappearances, i.e. the so-called National Reorganisation Process. But on 31 March 1982, the popular slogans resounding in the Plaza de Mayo during the huge demonstration convoked as the repudiation of the military government's economic policy already contained some indicators of the imminent military conflict.

"Peace, bread, and work" was the slogan that united the CGT organisers. The demonstration ended with the arrest of over a thousand people (the official figure). In a statement to the press, CGT maintained that Argentina was experiencing one of the gravest crises in its history and openly called for the restoration of democracy as it asked for a social act of solidarity: "'We, the united citizens, salute the beginning of actions which will lead us, thanks to the unity of the nation, to the overthrow of the Process and beginning of the road to happiness for the Argentine people."

> In the Plaza de Mayo, the crowd shouted, "Argentina! Argentina", "They must go!", "We want jobs", and "Down with the military dictatorship!": but the following eloquent slogan could already be heard: "If they're so brave (the military), let them go fight the British and the Chileans!" (*Clarín,* 31 March, "Several incidents and over a thousand people arrested during the repression of the demonstration.")

How did the media present itself during the conflict and what role did textual sources play? As of 30 March, *Clarín* placed the British press's view of the repercussions of the political-diplomatic escalation on its front page agenda (*Clarín*, 30 March, "Press commentaries" and "British good humour"). By 31 March, the rumour was already circulating that British nuclear submarines were being sent to the Argentine coast. This star position of the press – Argentine and British – whose primordial function was to inform about the imminent invasion, became determinant in the narration of the backdrop of the Argentine landing:

> The episodes that took place during the strained vigil indicate that in official circles the situation between the Argentine and British governments, after the events that occurred on 19 March in the Malvinas, are reaching a point of maximum tension. *Clarín* was able to verify that at 19:15 hours yesterday Vice-Admiral Juan Lombardo, commander of naval operations, travelled to the naval base at Puerto *Belgrano*. (*Clarín*, 1 April, "Worsening of the crisis with Great Britain: decisive hours".)

It is interesting to observe the account that the Argentine press made of the *Financial Times* commentaries, according to which the danger existed that the Argentine government could "fall prisoner to its own rhetoric" because, for the first time after seven years of silence, a strong opposition against the military government had appeared, or because the Military Junta was using the conflict with Great Britain as a "dissuasive tactic" against internal pressure. *Clarín*, citing the British newspaper, affirmed that "The Argentine government hears the diffused sense of nationalism and has a deeply rooted certainty, that the Falkland islands, called the Malvinas by the Argentines, belong to Argentina » (*Clarín*, 1 April, "Bellicose language in the British press").

The press's activity was marked with precision – identifying times, places and events – along with different modalities of newspaper work: "As this edition is going to press, the landing in Port Stanley, capital of the Malvinas, by Argentine troops is considered imminent. The action's objective is to recuperate the Southern territory occupied by Great Britain since 1833" (*Clarín*, 2 April, "The Argentine fleet deployed in the Malvinas").

> At 20:00 hours, the Secretary of Public Information held a press conference. Upon being asked if he foresaw freezing national television and radio, he responded, "Not at this time." Faced with

the possibility or a long wait, the Secretary admitted that press personnel should remain at their stations until the following morning. At 22:00 hours, sandwiches and beverages were served to accredited reporters on the first floor of the Government House. Everything indicated that important news was imminent. As the minutes passed, there was the insinuation that official announcements were late in coming; the wait seemed to project itself into a night-long venture. (*Clarín*, 2 April, "An agitated day")

The media's limelight position reached its apex at 10am on 2 April, when radio and television transmitted the first communiqué by the Argentine Military Junta. It stated that a combined action by the three branches of the Armed Forces had initiated a landing and initial combats to recover the Malvinas, Georgia, and Southern Sandwich Islands.

Clarín reported:

"Today has been one of unusual happiness. People only had eyes to read, with great interest, the headlines of the morning papers, which referred to the recuperation of the Malvinas, part of our national patrimony. The radio only had one news story to diffuse. The events occurred quickly and the result of the action was awaited with impatience. [...] Since it was taken as certainty that President Galtieri would address the nation, just as *Clarín* had predicted, two hundred people had already gathered in the Plaza de Mayo this morning." (*Clarín*, 3 April, "Popular support for the re-capture of the Malvinas")

This was how *Clarín* began the narration of the events. Emphasising the star role of the media in news crossovers ("the headlines of the morning papers", "the radio", "just as *Clarín* had predicted") it thereby places itself as a primary and active information source. It is only secondarily that the newspaper gives the floor to its other information sources and the event's protagonists. *Clarín* constructs the story and tells us:

It was 7:30 in the morning when an emergency meeting of the presidential cabinet was called by General Leopoldo Fortunato Galtieri. Present at the meeting were General Benjamín Menéndez, commander of the operation and the Armed Forces, and the Military Governor of the Malvinas. With a categorical "Good morning, Argentines" Galtieri began the meeting. Chancellor

Nicanor Costa Méndez gave his report about the important measures that had been taken. (*Clarín*, 3 April, "Popular support for the recapture of the Malvinas")

La Nación's way of treating the information in these first reports about the Argentine landing is radically different from *Clarín*'s enunciative strategy. In an opposition that we can call "protagonism versus neutrality", *La Nación*'s information produced a complementary effect. The tone of the information was impersonal and neutral. The journalist entered the scene only as a stylistic and narrative effect. Unlike the operation of "live transmission" produced when reading *Clarín*, *La Nación* elected to use the strategy of simultaneously presenting all the actors involved in the events. As an observer and "neutral" narrator, the newspaper reserved the articulation of sources through an indirect discourse style. Let us see how this enunciative strategy of neutrality works:

Argentina and Great Britain broke diplomatic relations yesterday and Chancellor Costa Méndez travelled last night to New York to defend our country's position in front of the United Nations' Security council, whose deliberations were being reinstated as this edition went to press. After the re-conquest of the insular territory that was solidified yesterday at dawn, the government of the Armed Forces is now ready to fight an international diplomatic battle in order to achieve in this domain that which has been achieved through direct action after 150 years of unfruitful negotiations with the United Kingdom and despite American pressure on Argentina to avoid the use of force. (*La Nación*, 3 April, "Citizens cheered by the re-conquest of the Malvinas")

In this brief narration, the attention is focused on the two collective principal actors, Argentina and Great Britain, while the person of Chancellor Costa Méndez, who would find in the future a large amount of reporting on his actions in this newspaper, is clearly delineated. Unlike *Clarín*, which calls military protagonists by name, *La Nación* indicates them by using the collective identifier "Armed Forces". The introduction of a third party in the dispute, the United States, gives the reader a general panorama of the powers in play. Information sources are evidently institutional and official here. The only reference to media protagonism is the citation of the temporality of the journalistic practice, "as this edition goes to press", which marks a type of task more than an information source.

The journalist's place is not one of direct information protagonist as in *Clarín*. Instead, he gives "testimony" to a piece of information that must circulate, of which he is not the direct producer. The journalist mediates between the "world" and the readers. The information is constructed "somewhere else" and *La Nación* brings it closer to the reader. The choice of this strategy freed the newspaper to adopt a "penetrating" narrative style that let the reader know the backdrop of what was occurring.

As a "testimony-giver", *La Nación* chose the account that enhanced its position not only as a newspaper close to power and information sources, but above all as an intermediary between the event and its reader. We will see how the narration continued, presenting journalists only secondarily as having an equivalent relationship to the public, but without losing awareness of the story that was developing before its eyes and the newspaper's mediator role:

> The events which took place yesterday in the Malvinas have naturally and necessarily produced an effect at the British Embassy, which occupies a large building in Barrio Norte [upper class neighbourhood in Buenos Aires]. As of dawn, diplomatic officials of the United Kingdom, journalists, and the curious lived the moments during which history was being made with disconcerting tranquility. From that moment, a large lapse of time passed, during which, like a strange omen, the British flag, the Union Jack with its central shield, languidly drooped in the calm and still morning air. At that moment, events that were unimportant became significant. (*La Nación*, 3 April, "The British Embassy or the mirror of a mute combat")

These first descriptions differentiate viewpoints, language choices, the importance given to various protagonists, the chorus of voices that rose up, and the press's activity. Later, the differences in these strategies would become more accentuated. Let us take the example of how Britain's response to the Argentine government was treated:

> British Chancellor Lord Carrington announced today in a press conference that his government had ordered the rupture of diplomatic relations with Argentina given the situation in the Malvinas. [...] The Chancellor – accompanied by Defence Minister John Nott – explained that the delay of information about military operations had been caused by the impossibility of communicating by telephone with the Malvinas. [...] In a later statement sent to the

BBC that responded to the possibility of Great Britain engaging in a war against Argentina, Nott said: "I hope not." (*Clarín*, 3 April, "London breaks diplomatic relations with Argentina")

From Her Majesty's Foreign and Commonwealth Office, the Secretary of State greets the Argentine Embassy's business minister and informs him that, given the Argentine invasion of the Falkland islands and the dependent British territories, Her Majesty's government is breaking diplomatic relations with the government of the Argentine Republic. In such circumstances as these, the Argentine Embassy's business *attaché* and his staff should leave the United Kingdom as quickly as possible and, under any circumstance, no later the midnight, April 9th, 1982. (*La Nación*, 3 April, "Great Britain breaks diplomatic relations")

The textual transcript of the official letter with which Great Britain broke diplomatic relations with Argentina was published in its entirety on *La Nación*'s front page, without comment. *Clarín,* though, continued to use its strategy of putting the media into the limelight and reporting what British officials said "live". The "world" enters into *Clarín* and goes out to the readers, but gives the readers the illusion that they were there together when it happened.

Asked about his own version of the events narrated by both newspapers, the then business minister for the Argentine Embassy in London, and present ambassador Atilio Molteni, told this author what he experienced on 2 April in London:

I was in London, charged with running the Argentine Embassy, when, on April 2nd, Chancellor Costa Méndez telephoned me. He told me that at the very moment he was calling me (9am London time) Argentine forces were landing on the Malvinas. There had already been indicators that the situation was about to reach a breaking point. I had received instructions form the Chancery – as shown in the Franks Report – to attempt to obtain a response from the British government to the treaty proposal that Argentina had presented in New York during February of 1982. In my conversations with British Foreign Officer Ferns, who was responsible for Latin American relations, it did not appear to me that the British had any intention of changing their attitude. I interrupted negotiations at the order of the Chancellor.

I thought that what would happen at that point was what was supposed to have happened, in other words, a confrontation on the

Georgia Islands and an escalation of the conflict. Instead, what occurred was an invasion of the Malvinas and this let Great Britain declare Argentina as the aggressor! On the Georgia Islands the situation would nave been different since we were authorised to be there. The Argentine landing changed the rules of the game and, in my opinion, was a mistake.

The previous Friday – 29 March – there had been a meeting at the Foreign Office, during which I suspected that the British had guessed something was going on. I had indicators that the British wanted to negotiate. Then Reagan called Galtieri, but it was already too late. Nobody could stop the Argentine Navy from going to war.

On the morning of 2 April, I was called by the Foreign Office and given an official appointment for 5pm I had no idea what would happen. They handed me an official letter rupturing diplomatic relations. It gave me until Thursday to leave London. I went back to Argentina on 9 April, after having received formal notification from the British government of the rupturing of relations. In a meeting with the Chancellor (Costa Méndez), I gave him my opinion which was that the English would fight us down to the last man. The Chancellor responded that he didn't see things the same way given the risk Great Britain ran in the cost of mounting such an operation. My opinion, though, was based on Margaret Thatcher's character, the interest of the British Navy to justify its existence and its role in preventing a future cutting of funds from the Navy's budget. And this was my report to the Chancery. (Interview with Ambassador Atilio Molteni, former Minister at the Argentine Embassy in London, 19 December 1990.)

A news report results from the "cutting-out" or segmentation procedure that journalists perform as a function of the ideology that each media holds over its own journalistic practice.

From the very beginning, the US intervention in the matter signalled enunciation differences between the press's "protagonism versus neutrality" strategies which characterised the beginning of the narration about the Argentine landing. While *La Nación* always maintained an impersonal and distant register, presenting the story under the title "The United States asks Argentina to withdraw its forces", *Clarín* presented it on its first page with a direct reporting style: "Reagan: 'I didn't think they'd do it.'"

The media story that best represents both a reality effect and the British information strategy in a situation of censorship is the transcript of the last official telex sent by the British government from Port

Stanley on the day of the Argentine landing that *Clarín* gave to its readers:

> London: What are all these rumours about?
> Port Stanley: We have a lot of new friends.
> London: What about the rumours of an invasion?
> Port Stanley: Those are the friends I'm referring to.
> London: Are they landing?
> Port Stanley: Of course.
> London: Are they open to traffic?
> Port Stanley: We still don't have any orders: we have to obey orders.
> London: Whose orders?
> Port Stanley: The new government's.
> London: Argentine?
> Port Stanley: Yes.
> London: The Argentines in the government?
> Port Stanley: Yes. You can't argue with thousands of soldiers when we're only 1800 strong. Stay on the line please. (*Clarín*, 3 April, "Last telex from Port Stanley")

The Construction of Media Truth

Blackouts, Denials and Secrets

Revelations, Denials and Spies

By using the media as a direct textual information source and by making reference to its own activity, *Clarín*'s and *La Nación*'s opposing narrative programmes can be established. We saw that *Clarín* elected to present the news of the Argentine landing from an enunciative position of "live" representation that reflected televised news reports. In fact, as a meta-enunciator, the newspaper often used direct quotations on its front page, thereby seeking identification with readers as they interpreted their feelings and formulated questions. In this way, the newspaper created a two-fold internal legitimisation, legitimising the reader through the legitimacy of its own enunciative activity. The timing of the public's expectations fused with, and corresponded to, the timing of the newspaper's enunciation, and consequently the timing of the story in which events were unfolding. The illusion of "being there" complemented the newspaper's strategy to present itself as a direct source of the reality narrated by its discourse. In its choice of enunciative frame, *Clarín* founded its media contract on its own enunciation and its star position as an information source of the story.

La Nación obscured this media stardom and relied on a standard news discourse: part "testimony-giver", the journalist fulfilled the enunciative task of delivering the information while adding a few selected elements. Through this meta-enunciator, the reader obtained a group of identifying details about journalistic practice – hours, movements, emotions – that let the reader form a precise sense of the events. In the construction of its media contract, *La Nación* sought a referential "information" illusion in which the story was written somewhere else (New York, London, or the Chancery) outside of the reader and media who heard (or saw) the story and relayed it.

In essence, the media performed a two-fold movement. *Clarín*, giving everyone the possibility to speak "live" chose the Media in the story. *La Nación*, showing us the limitations of its range, chose the position of the media as a witness of History. In their attempts to be legitimised, the newspapers made reference to official or institutional sources, aside from relying on their own enunciative mechanisms. Textual elements from different sources were hidden behind the textual strategy of a general "umbrella", as in:

1. "The military government of the Malvinas [...] affirmed before leaving" (*Clarín*, 5 April).

2. "The adjunct minister of Foreign Relations, Richard Luce" (*Clarín*, 31 March).
3. "According to the communiqué, the Military Junta (*Clarín*, 31 March).
4. "White House press secretary, Larry Speaker" (*La Nación*, 3 April).
5. "According to the words of General Galtieri" (*La Nación*, 4 April)
6. "Pope John Paul II manifested his concern today" (*Clarín*, 3 April).

It is easy to delineate from these examples the simultaneous presence of textual sources having political roles (ministers, governors), power positions (the Military Junta), spokesmen (White House press secretary), and the personification of political power (Galtieri) or religious power (the Pope). By and by, the newspapers "officially informed", but the importance of the political figure was such that the role of being powerful shaded what was said. Their statements were sufficient to provoke the events that the news related, and this enunciative role is what I have pointed out as being the performative value of certain social roles.

Not all subjects are "apt" for news production and this detail is so important that the role of news "promoter" precisely indicates the confluence between institutional power and enunciative power. From this is derived the need some social actors have, such as those who want to gain access into the stage provided by the media, to provoke accidents or scandals so as to call attention to themselves. What, then, is the specificity of "official sources"?

1. "During a highly agitated emergency Council session, the British government announced today that an air and naval operation would begin Monday. Its objective would be to recover the Malvinas." (*Clarín*, 4 April "The British government send air and naval forces to the islands".)
2. "Last night, President Galtieri assured that the Argentine Republic, will engage in combat, with all of the means it has at hand, only in the event that it is attacked." (*La Nación*, 4 April, "If the Argentine people are attacked, the Argentine Republic will fight".)
3. "British Prime Minister Margaret Thatcher said today that she is adamant in her decision to re-take the Malvinas and added that one always runs risks when a dictator is not checked. When questioned about her resigning in the event that the mission

were to fail, Margaret Thatcher responded: 'I cannot envision a defeat given the type of fleet and the type of personnel that we have.' She quoted Queen Victoria, saying: 'Defeat? The possibility does not exist!'" (*Clarín*, 5 April, "I cannot envision a defeat".)
4. "Last night, Great Britain announced a naval blockade of the Malvinas to begin as of midnight on Sunday. It declared an area of 351 km around the archipelago as a war zone, thereby threatening to attack the Argentine ships in the contested area." (*Clarín*, 8 April, AFP, UPI, ANSA, AP, Reuters agencies, "Great Britain announces a naval blockade of the Malvinas").

This heterogeneous information material responds to what the reader has traditionally perceived to be information from official sources as, among other things, its falsehood seems unthinkable. Given the political power figures that announce it, we find a series of invariants in this material. First of all, it is possible to distinguish "official textual sources" from extra-official or "unofficial" ones. The former almost always represents a figure tied to a power macro-structure such as the State or the Church, while it is generally difficult precisely to identify the latter. In this way, the criteria for determining the specificity of "official" textual sources cannot be established from the content conveyed, but from actors' enunciation forms. The repetition of the same enunciative operation corresponds to the evident diversity of social actors.

On the one hand, as much as enunciators, these actors are always related to highly stable identification operations, or they represent collective nouns such as "Argentina" or "Great Britain", or they are identified as specifically qualified subjects, such as "Ronald Reagan, President of the United States" or "Margaret Thatcher, the Iron Lady", which became a classic reference to the Prime Minister. On the other hand, these actors are further identified by situating shifters: time (yesterday, today, etc.) and places (at Parliament, in the Government house, etc.). From a semiotic viewpoint, official textual sources generally carry out narrative programmes tied to simple present or past verbal forms ("said", "considers", "affirmed", etc.) ; opinion verbs including "to consider", "to confirm", "to affirm", etc.; and the use of particular performative verbs such as "to declare", "to inaugurate", "to name", etc. This constellation of verbal forms creates a field of effects which result from the conjunction of political action with enunciative action.

What functionality do these sources have inside the press's information machinery? Not only do they permit precisely identifying the persons in play, giving, as we saw, descriptions of their performances, but they are basically the only sources that can be replicated, that are able to "deny" and, above all, that are authorised to "prove". All of these are typical information practice actions.

If we observe the escalation of the statements in examples 1, 2, 3 and 4, we can note that sources' roles are tied to a discursive interaction – in this case a polemic one – and a combination of strategies and movements determined not only by the source's position on the power ladder, but also by their position as a privileged source. Official textual sources "converse" among themselves through the media. The status of conversing is possible because official textual sources' positions are always symmetrical and equivalent. No official sources would lower themselves to rebut an unofficial source such as "military experts" or "another source from the Chancery". In part, this is because the latter are neither strongly visible nor identifiable, but above all they cannot be situated within any social and power reference structure. It is official textual sources' hierarchy that allows establishing the complementary or symmetrical rituals of dialogue.

What provokes the escalation effect in the preceding examples is the symmetrical attitude adopted by the Argentine and British governments. This attitude would continue throughout the Malvinas-Falklands conflict. Official textual sources' articulation reveals the newspapers' internal hierarchy in the structure and trust given to the enunciators. There are no significant differences between *Clarín*'s and *La Nación*'s manner of presenting sources. In both papers, a standard formula is used: *identification shifter + situating shifter*. What does vary is each newspaper's percentage of using sources. While *La Nación*'s use of official textual sources reached 24.24%, occupying second place behind the newspaper's own sources, *Clarín*'s use of official textual sources reached 13.84%, occupying third place behind unofficial sources. We can recall that for both newspapers the first textual source cited was the media. In other words, both newspapers' search for legitimisation was organised around substantiating their own discourse with institutional references (*La Nación*) and off-the-record information (*Clarín*).

Journalism's search for information, however, is not confined to the exclusive use of official textual sources. Within a general strategy of information production, journalism uses an information search tactic, a revelation of hidden truths tactic, a general tactic of seeking knowledge through clues and leads. Obviously, this information cannot appear under the title of "official textual sources". They are textual strategies in and of themselves and as such produce particular effects over readers. How can they be analysed and, most importantly, what do they represent? We can find examples in the first week of the Argentine-British conflict, when the British Task Force had not yet sailed from Plymouth, nor had it yet initiated the British naval blockade.

a) Hermeticism
1. "The Minister of Defence is maintaining the list of ships that are supposedly sailing toward the South in the most rigorous secrecy. In reality, not even official details exist about the fleet's size." (*Clarín*, 6 April, AFP, ANSA, AP, UPI and Reuters agencies, "The British fleet sails toward the South")
2. "These actions are being carried out in an atmosphere of hermeticism and discretion, despite the fact that some details are known." (*Clarín*, 4 April, the newspaper's own sources, "Washington's efforts")

b) Revelations
3. "A confidential report from the Atlantic Military Committee reveals doubts about the Atlantic strategies and the 'possibility of air-naval operation in the zone around the Malvinas'." (*La Nación*, 6 April, the newspaper's own sources, "NATO advises the withdrawal of the British Fleet")
4. "Despite the fact that there is no official information, it has been revealed that certain elements exist which can help reach a diplomatic solution." (*La Nación*, 7 April, the newspaper's own sources, "US manoeuvres for peace")

c) Denials
5. "The Minister of Foreign Relations has categorically denied a statement in a UPI dispatch sent by correspondent Irving Alcaraz [...] according to which Argentina has proposed to the United States that it install a naval base in the Malvinas." (*Clarín*, 4 April "Denial of information about the United States")
6. "In a press conference, British ex-governor Hunt declared that they were 'taken by surprise' by the landing on Friday in the archipelago, and that during the combat in Port Argentina (Formerly, Port Stanley) the Argentines had lost more troops than those reported in the official figures given by the government in Buenos Aires. 'Sailors killed five Argentines and not just one, as was reported.'" (*Clarín*, 6 April, AP, EFE,and Reuters agencies "According to the ex-governor there was more than one victim")
7. "Defence Minister John Nott indicated [...] that Great Britain

was putting together a fleet of forty warships, the most important fleet since the Second World War. But *The Daily Telegraph* reported today that the number of ships would be fewer and would reach an approximate total of twenty. [...] The Defence Minister has refused to deny the report." (*La Nación*, 6 April, Latin Reuters agency "Disagreement: are there twenty ships or forty?")

d) Spies

8. "According to a report today by the Times and *Daily Telegraph* in London, the British Secret Service agency that operates in Argentina maintains that it is possible that Great Britain will try to re-conquer the islands in the Southern Atlantic from the Georgias in order to pull the Argentine fleet into the high seas and sink it. This matches with the accounts of Buenos Aires' special envoys which appear in the newspapers. These envoys picked up the report that agents let the government in London know Argentina's intentions to recover the islands ten days before the landing. This makes the criticism of Margaret Thatcher ignore bitter reality. [...] According to dispatches, the secret agents maintain that one nuclear submarine could eliminate the entire Argentine fleet." (*Clarín*, 7 April, ANSA agency, "The opinions of the Secret Service are published")

9. "Lord Norton Hill [...] believes that 'the British fleet will have first hand information about the movements of Argentine ships thanks to satellite espionage, which will reach aircraft carriers by computer. It's also being said that the Argentines could take the islanders hostage in order to dissuade the British from a possible landing, but I believe that these reports are not based on fact. The Argentines are a civilised people and they do not want to appear treacherous in front of the entire world; with these lessons, the Argentines will come out smarting', says Norton Hill." (*Clarín*, 8 April, AFP, ANSA, AP, UPI and Reuters agencies, "Great Britain announces a naval blockade of the Malvinas")

Identity problems

Why are denials always "categorical" and hermeticisms always "total", and most importantly, how is it possible that spies appear in the newspapers when their existence and reports are a secret? Beyond the rhetorical clichés to which written information has habituated us, in practice a quarter of the information about the Malvinas-Falklands war that was published in the Argentine press fell into the category of either "denials", "revelations", or "secrets". The proliferation of contradictory information, i.e. denials; hidden information, i.e. revelations; or simply confidential information, i.e. secrets, poses the problem of extending the war concept to the press and highlights the conflictual and interactive dimension of the information concept. Some enunciative strategies, which I will analyse later, underline precisely this conflictual dimension of the press during a war situation.

Let us look at the case of the "denial". The social actor bases his or her identity on denying knowledge that is supposedly false and thereby creates controversy. This tactic, which is extremely common in war news and which we will see was used as a motive for sinking the British carrier *Sheffield* and the Argentine cruiser *General Belgrano*, is produced when at least two contrasting interpretations of an event are verified and, most importantly, when this information implicates at least two social actors who have access to the production of the news. The "denial" is an interaction between a minimum of two enunciative textual sources which find themselves in a symmetrical (true/false) and antagonistic position. They negotiate a specific knowledge from these positions from which will be constructed not only their own identities, but also a specific type of power: the power to account the truth.

In contrast, the "revelation" is not based on a negotiation between the truthfulness and untruthfulness of a piece of information. Instead, it is based on the dimension of the lie and the secret. Actors' "truth accounting" is not in play. What is in play is a system of distortion and hidden information to which this truth is submitted. The revelation, as Tuchman notes, is a reality construction strategy (Tuchman 1980: 178), that takes place through a group of reconsideration and revision operations. What is "revealed" is what manages to rise to the media's surface. In this case, an interaction was stabilised between textual sources taken as enunciation subjects who carried out a supplementary activity to that of "accounting." The media simply provided a place where this operation could find resonance. The interaction that was established was not symmetrical, as in the case of the denial, but complementary. The object of negotiating the information was not based on a specific or punctual action, but on a process of later revelations, which will always provide further details.

The explicit appearance of spies in the press tangentially touches the problem of sources' identities. The spy represents a two-fold strategy of hidden and altered identity. By definition the spy does not want to be identified. Consequently, in addition to his secret identity, he must have an alternative one under which to present himself. This operation is carried out as a secret: something that is real and true, but does not appear to be so. At the same time, the spy knows things that others don't know – and for this reason the spy can throw a government into crisis. The spy is paid to hide himself in order to obtain information. As in the revelation, the secret agent produces a particular type of knowledge but, unlike strategies that are related to the denunciation and its circulation; the knowledge produced by agents should not circulate. When the knowledge circulates, as in the case of the previously given examples, it is an exceptional instance in the media and is indicated as such. Spies' efficiency lies in their power to throw information fragments into the information arena, pace their circulation, and provoke the effect of surprise.

During the war, there were two exceptional cases in the press involving British and American spies. In their investigation of these cases, Gavshon and Rice affirm that, according to a report by British MP Tom Dalyell, the CIA had penetrated into Argentine military commands. During the Malvinas-Falklands war, the CIA was able to control the Argentine high command thanks to both their privileged access to important officials and to electronic communication devices (Gavshon and Rice 1984: 112). Hastings and Jenkins note that the British intelligence teams' landings in Argentina during the war were revealed to the entire world by the fall of a Sea King in Chile on 16 May. Task Forces were to deal with air threats in the Malvinas-Falklands and nowhere else (Hastings and Jenkins 1983: 184).

Personalisation versus Depersonalisation

Official textual sources, whose role, as we have seen, was to create an intertextual dialogue, have a high level of identification. Active unofficial textual sources, however, tend to diminish their level of personalisation and their actors become identifiable only through a generic grouping of shifters and pertinent elements:

1. "Argentine military sources have confirmed" (*Clarín*, 5 April).
2. "Military sources in London" (*Clarín*, 5 April).
3. "According to military experts" (*Clarín*, 7 April).

For their part, passive unofficial textual sources do not present any direct identification indices and express themselves in a completely impersonal manner:

1. "What is being said".
2. "It is known that".

3. "In well informed *milieux*".

In this way, active or passive unofficial sources make the possibility of verifying information extremely difficult. They become refractions of denials and, as such, are the space for proliferating information known as rumours, which I will analyse in detail in the next chapter.

Given that this type of source presents a relatively simple linguistic structure, their analysis poses the issue of their functionality in the production of "news about the Malvinas-Falklands". Let us consider the case of how the Argentine press narrated the British Task Force's deployment to the islands:

1. "The most important British war fleet to be constituted in the last twenty years finished its preparations today and sets sail tomorrow, Monday, for the Malvinas islands. In London, *military sources* have let it be known that the fleet is made up of thirty-six warships and two aircraft carriers — two-thirds of the British navy — and are transporting landing troops which, *according to press agencies*, oscillate between one thousand and three thousand men. [...] No comments have been made about the objectives set by the British authorities. *Military experts* are talking about three possible alternatives for the Task Force." (*Clarín*, 5 April, AFP, ANSA, EFE, TELAM and Reuters agencies "A strong naval contingent sets sail today from Great Britain")
2. "Amidst the emotional farewells and patriotic singing of thousands of people assembled here, the first ships set sail from this port with the objective of recuperating the Malvinas. The fleet forms part of the most powerful British armada since the Suez Canal crisis twenty-six years ago. With the aircraft carrier the *Invincible* at its head, it may have to confront Britain's first open sea battle since the Second World War in order to recover the Southern Atlantic colony taken last Friday by the Argentine army." (*La Nación*, 5 April, AP agency, "The British fleet sails toward the South Atlantic")
3. "*According to experts in maritime affairs cited today by the Washington Post*, British naval forces will not be able to carry out any important actions in the area of the Malvinas islands." (*Clarín*, 5 April, AFP agency, "Expert opinions")
4. "'We are not underestimating the enemy. British sailors are excellent professionals and they know it. Furthermore, we have been trained according to their naval tradition,' *said a qualified official of our navy*." (*La Nación*, 8 April, the newspaper's own

sources, "Strengths and weaknesses of the British fleet")
5. "*Military sources informed* that the military committee [...] has concluded that, in negotiations with Haig, we will consider negotiating everything except the sovereignty of the recovered islands. *Military spokesmen said that* Argentina will not abandon the Malvinas." (*Clarín,* 9 April, the newspaper's own sources, "Old objectives")

This series of news stories referring to one subject – the deployment of the Task Force in order to begin the naval blockade of the Malvinas islands, and subsequently the action's repercussions and evaluation – was presented in the Argentine press's agenda through agency dispatches, citations from other media, and the newspapers' own sources, during a four day period that ran from 5 April, the day the British fleet sailed, to 9 April, the eve of US Secretary of State Alexander Haig's first visit to Buenos Aires. As of this date, the subject lost importance, but did not entirely disappear from the newspapers' agendas. It was eclipsed by the attention the press gave to the US emissary's diplomatic efforts and Argentina's, personified here by the responses of Foreign Affairs Minister Nicanor Costa Méndez.

This series, which forms what I call a "micro-plot", constituted a veritable information flux, given the abundance of issues offered and the space accorded by the media agenda. In the newspapers, the story was told by exclusively unofficial textual sources, both passive and active. This is why these sources' functionality becomes a key question. Were there Argentine interests in the declaration that "we are not underestimating the enemy?" Did Argentina want to highlight its level of professionalism? Were there British interests in directly threatening Argentina with the power of a fleet that was equivalent to the one used in the Suez Canal crisis? Given that Haig travelled to Buenos Aires with the objective of conciliating conflicting interests, were there American interests in engineering a possible solution to the conflict? The fact that the press chose exclusively to use unofficial sources indicates a fog around the identification of the interests at stake.

The functionality of sources
As such, it becomes evident that these sources' function was to circulate information that could not be verified. What circulated was not necessarily an "official" piece of information, but one that could be considered to be credible. This credibility was transmitted to the reader through the pacifying figure of the "expert" and through the interaction of a group of "opinions" offered by the latter. The legitimisation of the

information was carried out by this designated textual agent who was never specifically identified ("the expert"), but – and here lies the paradox – thanks to his or her redundant presence, produced the effect of "knowledge" shared by the press and the readers.

At an international press level, the use of agency dispatches reveals the delineation of two interpretative configurations that were translated into two complementary information strategies: for the Americans, who sought a diplomatic solution to the conflict, it was necessary to prepare the field of national and international public opinion through Haig's visit and, for the British military, it was necessary to justify the Task Force's deployment to the Malvinas before its own public. These are complementary strategies because they reinforce the United States' dissuasive stance before the Argentine government on the eve of Haig's visit and Britain's dissuasive action, which began with the naval blockade whose most evident consequences for the Haig mission was the impossibility of negotiating when Argentine troops were found on the island and British ships were simultaneously threatening them. This news *cul-de-sac* was not resolved, and the Argentine strategy of presenting all of these contrasting voices was pedagogically functional to the formation of national public opinion.

If the functionality of this information flux is clarified when we consider that British news interests are in a double information loop, then what is the functionality of using unofficial textual sources in the Argentine press? First of all, it informs. An interpretative hypothesis can also be attempted: this type of news presentation tended to influence different lobbies in the Armed Forces and the diplomatic corps by presenting its spokesmen in solid positions, while also paving the way for the Argentine public's legitimisation of a diplomatic action.

For this reason, *Clarín* and *La Nación* preferred to use their own newspaper sources through the unofficial information of the Argentine navy's spokesmen in order to present the Navy's position about the limits of the negotiation that Argentine government could accept, or in reality the amount of power that the Navy had in the Military Junta. It is interesting to compare these Argentine press news strategies with the British press's ones. The best synthesis is presented by Hastings and Jenkins (1983), who argue that the tabloid press, with the exception of the *Daily Mirror*, filled its pages with practically historical headlines. Examples of this included those pointing to Haig's "duplicity" in the *Daily Mail* and the "refusal to surrender" commanded by the *Express*. The *Sun* relied on obscenities to refer to one of the peace proposals. The British Navy called for an old-time naval battle while the suspicion was growing that the Foreign Office was conspiring to avoid one.

Hastings and Jenkins give a series of succulent examples, such as the *Daily Star*'s desire to finish the political war, or the *Sun*'s declaration that the war had already begun on the day that the Task Force sailed. Despite this, publications such as the *Observer, The Financial Times* and *The Sunday Times* believed the dissuasive action of the Task Force. In accordance with *The Sunday Times*, a counter-invasion of the islands would be a blood-letting disaster. *The Financial Times*, which could not support the idea of a Task Force's existence, was inclined towards economic pressure. In the serious press, *The Telegraph* and *The Times* were the only supporters of the expedition, while *The Guardian* was a determined opponent (Hastings and Jenkins 1983: 156-57).

Internal or external dissuasion strategies refer to the group of operations that attempt to foresee potential enemies' reasoning due to the fear that the enemy will make a hasty and irresponsible decision. Because newspapers are basically huge intertextual machines that function under a memory made up of texts and days, reviewing *Clarín*'s and *La Nación*'s editorials and commentaries validates my first hypothesis: an initial military operation took place as a preparation for a later negotiation with Great Britain, an interpretation that history later proved to be false. In any event, as of the first week of the conflict, the news war had already exploded.

Truth and Credibility

As we have already seen, the news discourse's media contract operates from a "truth pact" with the reader. It is only Grice's *felicity condition*, i.e. the condition through which the pact can be carried out, which gives the discourse a credibility dimension. A news discourse cannot tolerate not being taken as "true" and in this sense it shares the political discourse's horror of being misunderstood. From this position, we can derive the need to establish a complex mechanism of reference indices. This mechanism is preferably organised around operations of presenting textual sources in order to create a cognitive effect: the production of high level knowledge which moves from the "certain knowledge" generated by the use of official textual sources, to "uncertain knowledge" produced by the use of unofficial ones.

War correspondents have the complex role of classifying these options in their discourse, but the readers are not in a position to check them. Rumours, denials and revelations break the linearity of the information, i.e. that utopian pretension of establishing a linear causality made up of pure visibility, by incorporating doubts and blackouts. The reader can choose between the different positions the media contract offers to run the road of the truth, secrets, lies, and falsehoods as discursive dimensions. In this way, the newspaper becomes a system of diverse and divergent, simultaneous and contradictory texts that do not communicate under a single register and within a sole parameter, but do so through parallel, and above all intertextual, systems.

I believe that these construction and presentation strategies of textual sources are in the order of news production because they attempt to delineate and negotiate the enunciator's legitimacy through the construction of his identity. This identity is based – given that it deals with the news genre and not with poetry or theatre – on a knowledge that is transmitted and negotiated and on a constant interaction between enunciative roles.

Official textual sources and revelations, denials and rumours are one of the parallel and complementary functions on which the logic of news production is based in a consumerist society. They are also reciprocally dependent since they auto-legitimate themselves. A news media that is only constructed from official source information could be justly accused of being pro-government and would produce the contrary effect to "objective" information by becoming hardly credible. A news media constructed without any evidence or strong anchoring reference, however, can be perceived as forming part of an exclusively fictional contract, which the news genre rejects. For a news media to be credible, it seems that it is necessary for it to present an even combination of these two news truth enunciation systems.

THE LIFE, PASSION AND DEATH OF A RUMOUR

The Story of the *Superb* Submarine

What happens when two orders of verisimilitude, i.e. official and unofficial sources, meld together using the press as their crucible? A possible media world is created of such strength and mastery as to be able to modify the course of the "real world".

On 31 March, the *Clarín* reader sees an article date-lined London. The piece is based on two telex reports sent out by Spain's EFE and France's AFP. The information contained in the telexes originates from ITV, Britain's privately owned television station. According to the televised report, "The British Navy has sent a nuclear submarine to the Southern Atlantic".

The announcement, reported by the war correspondent, includes the information that the submarine left its military base at Gibraltar for an unspecified destination. *Clarín* prints the story with the headline: "London has sent submarines".

This initial chain of inter-media back-and-forth which, as we have seen, is a characteristic form of legitimising the press, uses the media itself as its source. The report prompts the British Foreign Office to hold a press conference. The Office's press secretary announces that there is no official comment regarding the story: "We have nothing to say about the reported version." In response to journalists' questions about the submarines armament status, the press secretary responds that it is not armed with nuclear warheads.

This first declaration by the Foreign Office during the construction of the *Superb*'s possible media world highlights the issue of presuppositions in press information. Consequently, all belief about the truthfulness of the information is suspended and, so, the reader can consider it to be a "version".

The report, however, has already entered into the arena of media circulation. The reader, thus, has at least four pieces of information:

1. a submarine called the *Superb* exists;
2. it is a nuclear submarine;
3. it is not currently equipped with nuclear warheads;
4. it has left its base at Gibraltar for an unspecified destination.

The possible media world has supplied its Model Reader with a series of properties necessary for the correct identification of the semantic unit "nuclear submarine". It thus transforms it into a textual topic, and at the same time, it transforms the empirical reader into a Model Reader, because simultaneously the reader is now in a position to exercise "conjectural thinking" (Eco 1990: 236) and can clearly infer four pieces of complementary and intertextual information. This information will begin to delineate a media world through which will navigate the reader's belief that:

1. the nuclear submarine *Superb* is heading towards the Malvinas-Falklands;
2. no information has been published about its exact armament status because it is a military secret;
3. the news story is treated as a "version" precisely because it is a leak of classified military information;
4. something important must be in play if the British Foreign Office is making statements concerning the report.

The reader can also generate an interpretative or hypo-codified abduction such as "given the diplomatic escalation of the Argentine-British conflict, it's possible that nuclear submarines are being used". The reader might also decide to subscribe to an explanation strongly supported by the media's inter-transmission: "If British television, an Argentine newspaper and two international press agencies from countries not even directly involved in the conflict are giving out the same report *that no one denies*, then there's a good chance that it's true."

On the following day, 1 April, while awaiting the Argentine landing on the Malvinas-Falklands, *Clarín* increases the tension level with an article entitled "Worsening of the crisis with Great Britain". The newspaper credits itself with the 31 March news-piece:

> Sources consulted by *Clarín* have confirmed that Williams (the British ambassador to Argentina) has been called by the Argentine Chancery. Referring to the report that the British government has sent a nuclear submarine to the conflict zone, he stated: "I can only respond to questions concerning diplomatic matters, not military operations."

The suspense signal emitted by the newspaper gives the Model Reader a preview of the future development: either the possible media world will be confirmed or refuted. Either action will carry with it corresponding propositional attitudes.

Confirmation is not long in coming. In an article appearing on page four the very same day, *Clarín* uses unofficial sources in its article "The deployment of British ships to the Malvinas-Falklands is confirmed". The paper reports that five telexes datelined London indicate that AFP and EFE's 31 March cables had been picked up by three other international agencies: Italy's ANSA, the US's AP, and Britain's Latin Reuters. The reader has no reason to doubt that these world famous information agencies have already checked corresponding sources.

The reader goes on to see that these agencies confirm the *Superb* as being "a nuclear fuelled submarine, which has left its base in Gibraltar and is heading for the Malvinas-Falklands". An important piece of information is added: the submarine weighs 4,500 tons and its crew of 97 is specialised in submarine detection. The submarine's possible media world is then furnished with new elements: it is also reported that "a second Hunter-Killer class submarine, as well as several other frigates and aircraft carriers, may accompany the *Superb*" (*Clarín*, 1 April "The deployment of British ships is confirmed").

At this point, the experts intervene. From the International Institute for Strategic Studies in London, top British specialist Mayor Elliot deems the deployment of Hunter-Killer class nuclear submarines to be a highly efficient measure: "With government authorization, the *Superb* would be capable of rapidly sinking two to three Argentine naval units."

Another newspaper, Britain's *Daily Telegraph*, also steps in. While relating the characteristics of the submarine's crew, the paper hints that the ship *is currently in the area of the Malvinas-Falklands*: "The submarine crew stationed in the islands' waters pertains to an 'élite' group of the Royal Navy" (*Clarín*, 1 April, "The deployment of British ships is confirmed"). Using the original two telexes from EFE and ANSA datelined London, it affirms that: "Yesterday, all British newspapers reported the deployment of a nuclear submarine to the Malvinas-Falklands" (*Clarín*, 1 April, "Bellicose language in the British press").

The nuclear submarine delineated by the possible media world does not pertain to the real world experience of the reader who has probably never seen a British nuclear submarine. It can, however, enrich the reader's intertextual and encyclopaedic experience as a model media reader. "A narrative world borrows properties from the real world. In order to do this without wasting energy, the narrative world activates individuals already recognised as such. The narrative or possible world does not necessarily reconstruct these individuals element by element. [...] A possible world greatly overshadows the real world of the reader's encyclopaedia" (Eco 1979: 131).

As such, technical verification of the story becomes momentarily unnecessary. The story has been amply guaranteed by the experts. The possible media world constructed need only be sufficiently probable and credible for the model media reader to accept it. At this point, he is already capable of interpreting the totality of information received about the submarine and can this filter it into a personal frame of reference as a "small world".

Within 24 hours the initial story has entered the category of certainty. The story becomes credible not only because of the amount of identifying signs that allow the reader to imagine the submarine in detail, but also because of the resonant echo from other media which reconfirm the reader's initial abductions. To these abductions must now be added the reader's fear that the submarine, which has advanced destructive power and speed, is practically on Argentina's doorstep. These inferences place into motion not only a system of logical expectations but also, and above all, emotional ones.

What truly strengthens the model media reader's belief in the existence of the submarine are official statements by British Defence Minister John Nott. Asked by journalists to confirm or deny the *Superb*'s presence in the waters surrounding the Malvinas-Falklands, Nott states: "I do not comment on rumours" (*Clarín,* 1 April, "Absolute silence"). Herein is one of the paradoxes of strategic information: any other statement made by Nott would have been considered as false. But the very act of qualifying the story as a rumour highlights and strengthens the information without the necessity of overtly confirming or denying its veracity. Such is the power of lexical presuppositions.

The Argentines still had not landed on the Malvinas-Falklands when the British *counter-information strategy* was set in motion. This Argentine escalation, which permits a strategic production and diffusion of the rumour, parallels the intensity of the British retreat from the islands: on 2 April, not only was Port Stanley surrendered, thus signalling the high point of the British retreat, but the British flagship – the icebreaker *Endurance* – was the one to lead the withdrawal (*Clarín,* 2 April, "The British fleet operating in the Malvinas-Falklands-Falklands"). Does this action, which organises factual history in a particular way, signify the death of the rumour and the dissolution of the possible media world? Absolutely not. In the meantime, the rumour has already entered Argentina and now not only do newspaper sources contribute to its construction but so does "information from certain sources associated with the Argentine Defence Ministry, which state that nothing is known about the location of an nuclear submarine called the *Superb*, which London situates as being in the waters of the South Atlantic" (*Clarín,* 2 April, "The British fleet is operating in the Malvinas-Falklands"). The press, busy covering the Argentine landing on the islands, momentarily loses sight of the submarine's precise location. The model media reader has, though, already registered this new existing presupposition on the Argentine side, and the reader can legitimately become more and more nervous.

By 4 April, after the political-military shock of the Argentine invasion had lessened, the submarine returns to comply faithfully with the dictate that all creatures born in a possible media world must be fed and cared for:

> According to reliable military sources cited by AFP, a nuclear submarine, which may, or may not, be the *Superb*, has been sighted in international waters off the coast of Mar del Plata. It is sailing in the direction of the Malvinas-Falklands. (*Clarín*, 4 April "Two British ships?")[1]

Given the seriousness of the report, an Argentine reader exercising the power of critical interpretation could begin to feel that checking the "reliable military sources" is urgent: are they Argentine or British? How can a British nuclear submarine be only 600 kilometres from the Argentine capital? And furthermore, are there now two submarines? The possible media world offers nothing in response to these questions, but does momentarily calm the model media reader: safety measures have been ordered by the Argentine navy in all major sea resorts.

London, meanwhile, continues to carry out its strategy of planting presuppositions. Defence Minister John Nott repeats that he cannot confirm or deny if the *Superb* is carrying out operations off the Argentine coast: "I have no intention of giving any information about the location of our submarines" (*Clarín*, 4 April, "Two British ships?"). This is the third case of presuppositions that the British possible media world has presented. By maintaining his refusal to comment, Nott nourishes the suspicion that British submarines are actually off the Malvinas-Falklands. As opposed to the previous presuppositions conveyed by the Foreign Office and Nott, both of which characterise reports about the submarine as "versions" or "rumours", Nott's present intervention as an *active official source* closes the British information strategy circle in the construction of a possible media world and in the cooperative response to it awaited from the reader.

It seems clear that Nott's presupposition is meant to be inserted in

---

[1] Mar del Plata is a principal Argentine sea-resort, which could accommodate three million tourists at the time. It is located approximately 600 kilometres from Buenos Aires.

the already woven semiotic fabric as a pre-constructed discourse. If presupposition is always considered to be an anaphoric transmission, then it can also be considered to be the starting point of a cataphoric process. Nott's statement is a case of existential presupposition because it depends on a particular enunciation strategy.[2] As such, Nott's statement acquires a particular power, in as much as the statement's objective is, as shall be seen, effectively to convince the public that the British government has sent submarines to the Southern Atlantic. This enunciative power can be exercised not only because Nott has specifically referred to the rumour, but primarily because of his special position as an information source.. The entire socio-semiotic network supports him. His presupposition thus becomes highlighted information and is picked up by the papers, thereby activating the interpretative mechanisms of its model media readers.

A telex from London on 3 April disseminated by AP, EFE, Latin Reuters and American UPI – which up until now had not placed itself in the hunt for the submarine – throws the submarine's whereabouts into question. The report affirms that the *Superb* can be currently found at the head of a blockade Task Force navigating towards the Southern Atlantic (*Clarín*, 4 April "The British government sends an air-naval force to the Malvinas-Falklands"). The story, published by *Clarín* on page 18 on 4 April, throws the model media world which the reader has patiently constructed into turmoil: if the *Superb* is, as UPI reports, presently sailing towards the south, then what submarine is, as AFP reports, off the shores of Mar del Plata? Just how many submarines are there? British Prime Minister Margaret Thatcher intervenes in the possible media world indirectly to explain why a discursive fleet of phantom submarines is necessary and thereby to curb all possible doubt on the part of the model media reader as to the submarine's existence. On 3 April, Thatcher is attacked by the Labour party during a session in the House of Commons immediately proceeding the Argentine landing. While defending herself, the Prime Minister states: "It would be absurd to send the entire fleet every time Buenos Aires speaks aggressively" (*Clarín*, 4 April, "The British government sends an air-naval force to the Malvinas-Falklands"). While awaiting the British Task Force's arrival in the islands' waters, a fleet of obviously swifter rumours and

---

[2] "Existential presuppositions have the power of making their referential object existent, regardless of whether or not their existence has previously been known. The very act of mentioning it creates a propensity for existence" (Eco 1990: 300).

presuppositions can be deployed.

Only two days have passed since the Argentine landing. Why hasn't Argentina organised – either through official or unofficial media information sources – its own counter-information strategy? Because to respond to a presupposition one must first construct a complex counter-presupposition. The Argentine government, which lacked even a basic information strategy, simply failed to do this. Regardless, the possibility for the Argentine official sources to carry out a meta-discursive intervention existed. This intervention could have situated itself outside of the communication interaction, framing it: we have already seen how textual sources "talk" with each other. It could have attempted correctly to identify the nature of British information.

On Monday 5 April Argentine forces from the recently created Malvinas-Falklands Theatre Operations Command militarily reinforced the islands. Meanwhile, at Portsmouth, the British government moved her troops into its largest battle fleet assembled since the Second World War, and the DAN press agency tagged along in the hunt to find, and identify, the submarine. A DAN telex, published by *Clarín*, reports that the *Superb* is 250 kilometres from Buenos Aires and is heading directly towards the Malvinas-Falklands. In the possible media world, the story contributes to the construction of the submarine's identity as a textual topic by adding new characteristics:

1. the submarine has a particular speed;
2. it can remain submerged for long periods of time;
3. it has a special type of highly destructive torpedo (*Clarín*, 5 April, "A strong naval contingent leaves Great Britain today").

On Tuesday 6 April the Argentine Navy decides to enter the possible media world: they attempt unofficially to locate the submarine's position and identify her characteristics. Tracking the submarine through news pieces published after 31 March, and confirming its presence in the waters off Mar del Plata, the Navy signals that, "As of two days ago, the submarine should be in proximity to the islands." This temporal and spatial localising function ("as of two days ago" and "in proximity to the islands") includes an additional piece of information: an Argentine submarine, the *Salta,* is being deployed because of the *Superb*'s presence in international waters (*Clarín,* 6 April, "Military preparations off the Argentine coast").

To conclude the rumour's first week of life, Rodolfo Terragno, London-based correspondent of Venezuela's *El Diario*, intervenes in the international dialogue. In Caracas, *El Diario* publishes his report that the 4,500 ton nuclear propelled submarine called the *Superb* is presently in proximity to the Malvinas-Falklands; but this titbit of information is one with which the model media Argentine reader is already familiar.

The Proliferation of the Rumour
The rumour and conflict's second week begins with the introduction of the United States on the scene. Brandishing United Nations resolution number 502, the US assumes a negative diplomatic policy towards Argentina. The resolution requires that Argentina withdraw its troops from the islands. Secretary of State Alexander Haig begins travelling back and forth to Buenos Aires. The rumour's second week is rich in information about the submarine: there are now two of them, the *Superb* and the *Oracle*. This time, the possible media world binds itself to its previously constructed script and the model media reader need only activate the already delineated topic "nuclear submarine". Although the *Superb* still maintains its "nuclear" semantic property, the *Oracle* is a conventional, diesel-propelled unit.

The telex which heralds the news is simultaneously published in London, New York and Madrid by the AFP, ANSA, AP, EFE, Latin Reuters and UPI. To the existing data about mother *Superb* – 4,500 tons and a crew of 97 – must now be added the telexed information that she travels at a velocity of 30 knots per hour (explaining her speed in reaching the Malvinas-Falklands coastline after passing Mar del Plata only two days after her deployment from Gibraltar), and that she carries five 533 millimetre torpedoes. Her daughter, the *Oracle*, weighs 2410 tons, has an underwater speed of 17 knots, and a modest crew of 68. Despite her smaller size, the *Oracle*'s battle capacity is greater: she has eight 533 millimetre torpedoes. Evidently not satisfied with this little family, *The Times* affirms that four of the Royal Navy's nuclear submarines "are sailing to the islands of the South Atlantic" (*Clarín*, 8 April, "The advance of the British fleet continues").

Twenty-four hours before Alexander Haig's arrival in Buenos Aires, the submarines were identified by journalist Jacques Isnard of France's *Le Monde*. The report comes to the aid of the media world which has been created up until this point. *Clarín*, entitling Isnard's story "A submarine fleet!", also cites information from the *Times*' new article. *Superb*'s other children are called the *Sceptre*, the *Spartan* and the *Splendid*. Each weighs 4,500 tons and is armed with torpedoes valued for their silence. The model media reader, who has been following events daily, is alerted: "With such a submarine force, London will be using military means to implement the threatened blockade approved by the House of Commons on April 7th" (*Clarín*, 9 April, "A submarine fleet?").

The multitude of identifying signs, the testimony of the experts, the international agencies that simultaneously dispatch new information, the different telex datelines, the dialogue between newspapers and, finally, Argentina's unofficial statements alongside Britain's official ones, makes doubting the existence of British submarines in the South Atlantic difficult. The possible media world and the inter-media system that has sustained it have managed to construct something extremely tangible, real and credible: a family of nuclear submarines. The Model Reader has no escape.

Altered states

The newspaper itself starts to doubt the existence of the submarines at this point. *Clarín* leaves the evidence aside in order to conjecture:

> According to information from expert sources, the majority of the units in question could not reach the waters off the Malvinas-Falklands Archipelago for 10 days (after their deployment from Gibraltar). Despite this, all information leads one to suppose that Hunter-Killer nuclear submarines can already be found in the region. The British press frequently refers to four such units. (*Clarín*, 10 April, AFP, EFE and Latin Reuters, "British troops are reinforced")

Clarín's statement is important because it signals a weak point in the construction of the *Superb*'s possible media world: for one part, a hard nucleus of identifying signs continues to circulate. These signs assign properties given by British sources: nuclear power, speed, and crew. These signs, which will continue to circulate in the media, can be called PMW 1. For another part, PMW 2, in which certain properties of PMW 1 can be already found in the Malvinas-Falklands, are "narcotised".

If PMW 1 and PMW 2 are both states in the same possible media world ("the nuclear submarine *Superb*") then this point of temporal dysfunction in the newspaper ("in ten days") permits the model media reader to distance him or herself from the reported information and carry out a doxastic disconnection: "The possible submarine that has been delineated as an inhabitant in my world of beliefs may be the same entity within a real world or may be a different entity in a different world".[3]

---

[3] For an analysis of abductive phenomena, see Eco 1990: 22ff. They are mechanisms which create worlds.

The Life, Passion and Death of a Rumour

Argentina's Minister of Foreign Relations, Chancellor Nicanor Costa Méndez, its President, General Fortunato Galtieri, and the other two members of the Military Junta, Admiral Jorge Anaya and Brigadier General Lami Dozo, are unable to reach a negotiation agreement with U. S. Secretary of State, Alexander Haig. Haig travels to London on 11 April with Argentine's official proposal. The pause created by PMW 2 dissolves along with the possibility of a diplomatic solution. On the same date, *Clarín* offers new information:

> The British press echoes the analysis of some military observers who point out that Great Britain is likely to initiate a blockade with five nuclear submarines, four of which are presently to be found in the waters off the Malvinas-Falklands. These submarines will act alone while awaiting the British Task Force, which comprises 36 ships, and which was deployed-five days ago from Portsmouth and Gibraltar. (*Clarín*, 11 April, "Thatcher ratifies the blockade")

While the United Kingdom hardens its position in response to the Argentine conditions brought by Haig to London, the submarines become legion. *Clarín,* basing itself on its own sources, reports that, "According to certain rumours, and as London has warned, Soviet and U.S. submarines will be patrolling the waters off the Malvinas-Falklands" (*Clarín*, 12 April, "A peaceful vigil").

The Argentine reader finds himself or herself in a submarine war film. Historical events relate to the situation at hand: who can forget the *Graf Spee,* the German pocket battleship which, at the outset of the Second World War, came to die on the shores of Montevideo, scuttled after unrelenting pursuit? The reader already has so many analogous intertextual models. The possible media world sustained by *Clarín* permits the reader to select a group of interpretative hypotheses which operate like an economic principle. Given the persistence of historical imagery, the reader can expect the *Superb* to have the ability to unleash the Third World War as "there are those who remember that Germany's decision on 1 February 1917 to declare 'submarine war without restrictions' ultimately determined the United States' entry into the First World War" (*Clarín,* 12 April, "Britain begins a naval blockade in the Southern Atlantic").

But the reader must also contend with 12 April, the key date of both Alexander Haig's trip to London and the beginning of the British blockade. The reader can propose a group of hypo-coded abductions according to which "the interpretation has been selected as being the most plausible among others, but it is still uncertain whether it is or isn't correct. An explanation can only be given in consideration of successive verifications" (Eco 1991: 237). The reader can suppose, for example, that the story about the quickly identified British submarine fleet, which has been furnishing the possible media world, is being circulated simply to intimidate the Argentines. If this supposition is correct, then why has no Argentine information source unmasked the British strategy, by calling its bluff? Doing so would constitute an Argentine defence counter-information strategy.

From the British point of view, the issue was to construct a credible and effective information strategy. To do this, unofficial information had to be given out in London and then picked up and "owned" by the Argentine press. The model media reader, however, cannot discern the British counter-strategy, because no textual index in the possible media world has informed the reader about it. The reader might also implement a group of meta-abductions. Through these they can decide if the possible media world delineated by preceding inferences coincides with their universe of experience. The reader, however, cannot, *a priori*, brand *Clarín* as a traitor for having disseminated information that favoured the enemy's information strategy. The reader cannot label the newspaper as a turncoat, precisely because of the presence of an external media contract which: (a) includes a media trust construct permitting the newspaper's sale and consumption; and since (b) the newspaper includes other sections, such as editorials and articles about diplomatic negotiations that clearly signal the paper's support and defence of Argentine interests. What can the reader do?[4]

Hypothesis 1 or the negotiation supporters: some British and Argentine political sectors are interested in reaching a diplomatic solution. Nourished by newspaper articles published for approximately two weeks, which are based on the rumour that a submarine fleet is being deployed, and which alert both British and Argentine public opinion about the military, political, and life cost implied by a frontal encounter, interpretative hypothesis and plausibility is strengthened by

---

[4] The reader can, for example, stop reading *Clarín* and switch newspapers. *La Nación* published only three stories about the *Superb* during the same time frame. A small box on page 10 in their 3 April edition entitled, "At liberty to sink aircraft carriers" specifically refers to the *Superb*. Another small article on page 4, 13 April, entitled "So many submarines" counts the possible nuclear submarines circulating in the region, but makes no specific reference to the *Superb*. A final story on 20 April, published on page 2, "Alarm in the British fleet because of submarine", is dedicated to an unidentified submarine sighted 30 nautical miles from the British fleet.

the rumours' systematic persistence and by the lack of Argentine control over them. Here, there is a nuclear arsenal of such potency that it can only be vanquished by a peace agreement; it is fundamentally an invisible entity, a dissuasive and mythological submarine:

> As of daybreak four nuclear submarines have been operating in the blockade zone. The submarines have begun to send information to their admiral ship, the aircraft carrier Hermes. According to a British specialist, the submarines are a threat to the Argentine fleet. Their main advantage is that they can remain submerged for two months at a time and can navigate underwater at a speed above 30 knots an hour. The same expert affirms that this speed cannot be matched by Argentine surface ships. According to consulted sources, the British submarine's radars are highly superior to the Argentines'. All of them are equipped with Tigerfish Mark 241 torpedoes that can hit targets up to 17 miles away. Their radars benefit from the enormous energy of nuclear reactors and have a wider operating radius than that of Argentine surface ships and Argentine anti-submarine helicopters. The experts are convinced that the Tigerfish are capable of easily sinking Argentine vessels. (*Clarín*, 12 April, AFP, ANSA, AP, EFE and Latin Reuters, "The British fleet reaches Ascension Island")

Hypothesis 2 or the war supporters: other British and Argentine political sectors are uninterested in a United Nations-sponsored negotiated solution to the conflict. They want to construct a powerful counter-information strategy (disqualification of the enemy) that can be manipulated (proper qualification) in order to defeat the British.

The rigid position of both these sectors can be better understood in light of the fact their hypotheses were voiced between 12 and 14 April, i.e. exactly when Alexander Haig was in London delivering the Argentine peace proposal and ascertaining the British negotiation position.

> A press secretary for the Ministry of Defence confirmed yesterday that British submarines have been sent to the Malvinas-Falklands islands. This action is consistent with the reinforcement of the British blockade which began at daybreak on 12 April. Several reports, though, fail to coincide about the number of submarines in the blockade zone. [...] Hunter-Killer submarines, whose presence has not been denied by the British government, are among the most modern of their class. According to the British Admiralty, these

submarines are practically undetectable. Their radar system can locate enemy ships up to 40 miles away. Experts, however, do not underestimate the strength of Argentine forces, which is superior to that of any other Latin American nation. (*Clarín*, 13 April, AFP, ANSA, AP and Latin Reuters, "London confirms that submarines are patrolling the water off the Malvinas-Falklands")

According to a high ranking naval officer, Argentine defence forces have located British submarines off the Malvinas-Falklands. Their presence is not affecting regular airdrops to Argentine troops defending the island. Qualified naval sources indicate that four British submarines are enforcing the naval blockade. Of these, only two are nuclear units from the Hunter-Killer class. These units can be used to both detect and attack Argentine vessels. The Argentine Armada possesses a thousand planes, including Trackers and Neptunes, as well as ships which can locate enemy submarines. According to our sources, the enemy submarines have orders to blockade a highly defined and reduced area. (*Clarín*, 14 April, "Air-carrier deployment to the islands is confirmed, submarines have been detected")

The media holds a cancerous viewpoint, which can be labelled Hypothesis 3. It is possible that unverified information was passed back and forth within and between media and press agencies. Like a diseased cell, this information set off a multiplication process that became impossible to arrest. If this hypothesis is correct, then news was produced on the basis of published conjecture, instead of hard facts. The reader, accepting Hypothesis 3, would be freed from the ingenuous position which had been delineated for them, and would be placed instead in a critical extra-semiotic position. The reader would run the risk, however, of placing the established media contract with the press in general, and *Clarín* in particular, into crisis. Is it worth running such a risk?

The Death of the Rumour

Clarín was silent on 15 April. Coincidentally, this was the day that Haig arrived in Buenos Aires to deliver the official British response. On 16 April, telexes from AFP, ANSA, UPI and Latin Reuters begin to "narcotise" the submarine's aggressive profile, attributing simple "patrol" functions to it (*Clarín*, 16 April, "The British fleet undergoes exercises on the open sea"). On 17 April, an official Argentine Navy source commented that the British had excellent submarines "precisely because they cannot be located" (*Clarín*, 17 April, "Argentine ships sail towards the Malvinas-Falklands"). Given the amount of identifying signs that the *Superb* had left in her wake, the reader could now begin to suspect that she was a fake.

On 18 April, TELAM issued a telex. Datelined Rio de Janeiro, it reported that a Brazilian commercial airline pilot had sighted and photographed a submarine navigating in the Gulf of Santa Catarina, "but it is doubtful that the vessel can be correctly identified as poor meteorological conditions affected the quality of the photograph" (*Clarín*, 18 April, "Spotted in Brazil"). A rare event: a photograph of a rumour. The *Superb* deteriorates to the category of the Loch Ness monster, another often photographed rumour.

The submarine lost itself in the mist and failure of the Haig mission. The report on the 18 April was the last piece of information that the Argentine reader would have about the *Superb*. The presence of phantom submarines was now unnecessary as the British task force was only 80 kilometres away from the Georgia Islands. On 22 April, *Clarín* published the submarine's obituary, date-lined London, on page 6:

> A British submarine which was previously reported as patrolling the waters off the Malvinas-Falklands has been sighted in Scotland. The submarine appears to *have never been* in the South Atlantic. Defence sources confirmed today that the nuclear submarine *Superb* was presently returning to its home base of Faslane, off the river Clyde. (*Clarín*, 22 April, Latin Reuters, "It showed up in Scotland")

On 23 April, both the *Daily Record*, Scotland's most widely read newspaper, and regional television reported that the *Superb* had never left her home base. The British Defence Minister "is obliged to admit that a bluff has been discovered on the part of the British" (*Clarín*, 23 April, "The *Superb* bluff"). The submarine died as it had been born, through media intra-transmission.

Media Truth

The rumours and stories that circulated about the *Superb* step outside the bounds of journalistic propriety and enunciation. The question is not if the press did, or did not, knowingly lie. What must be analysed are the elements which permitted the *Superb* story to circulate as non-fiction, when it was really a fictional work. The story was framed in a kind of discourse which did not prevent the introduction of fictional elements. Let us look at some of these elements:

(a) The enunciator's viewpoint: the identity charade

The submarine story's identity is originally classified as "a reported version". In the construction of the possible media world of the *Superb*, it has already been seen how a group of indices which were fundamentally related to press agencies' textual sources allowed carrying out a precise identification: the submarine's identity is a "fact" because it was labelled as such by a varied group of social actors from different places.

A second level of analysis deals with the identity of the constructed object, instead of on the type of information which contributed to that construction. The official and unofficial textual sources which were repeatedly circulated throughout press agencies, as well as the expert opinions and statements collected about the submarine, agreed on a huge amount of semantic traits and qualitative identification elements assigned to the submarine.

A third level of analysis focuses on the identity of the object in relation to the power position of sources who made statements about it. The statements of the Foreign Office, British Defence Minister John Nott and Prime Minister Margaret Thatcher contain a special authoritative ring – they are, after all "official" sources – which contribute to frame the story as truth.

For a story to circulate as truth there must be social agreement about it. Because the *Superb* lie had a pragmatic value, constructing a consistent possible media world for it was essential. As such, a media contract became necessary.

(b) The reader's viewpoint: the possibility of proof

How strong is the argument that the information presented to the reader was credible? In other words, what guidelines did the reader use to decide to believe, or to not believe, the submarine identity statements made by the media? Classical research on media reception indicates how much the reader will trust information presented across different media formats as truthful (Gunter 1987; Wolf 1993). In relation to the analysis of true information presented about the *Superb*, it seems obvious that the reader was capable of developing personal verification hypotheses that could, or could not, be utilised. Although the media left some room for doubt, it did not give the reader decoding elements, nor did it assign the reader a precise physical location in which both the *Superb* and the reader's belief in it could reside.

It seems clear that any attempt by the reader to verify the *Superb* story implied, at the very least, an extra-semiotic operation in which the reader had to leave aside the report that the submarine had been found in Scotland. Such an operation, however, is a Epimenidian paradox: the operation is impossible because the 22 April report about the "real" *Superb*'s location inhabits the same possible media world as the rumour. In other words, the media world was transformed into a vicious circle: if the reader believed in statements which indicated that the *Superb* was off the Malvinas-Falklands coast for 20 days, then how could the reader simultaneously believe in statements by the same enunciative newspaper sources (the press agencies, John Nott, etc.) that throughout that same time frame, the *Superb* was in Scotland? How could the reader decide if the press was lying at the beginning or the end or vice-versa? From the reader's point of view, deciding what to believe and when was undecidable.

The *Superb* case is a salutary example of a rumour used in a psychological war strategy. It can also appear to the reader to be a case of "false information". Italian researcher Carlo Marletti, a well known specialist in analysis of fake information, writes of new journalism:

> Questioning the frontiers between reality and fiction [...] the new journalism has failed to give us any clue that is truly news or relevant for the redefinition of exchange relations and for the reciprocal relationship between fiction and reality which is in crisis. [...] The sociology of knowledge indicates that no manipulation or falsification can be effective in and of itself, but can only be viewed in relation to a defined "irreality construction" within which it acquires its own significance. [...] A falsehood, in other words, is "valued" only when conditions exist which make duplicity difficult. (Marletti 1984: 60-62)

Asked about why *Clarín* backed a story for over 20 days which was later discredited, journalist and editorialist Ricardo Kirschbaum, who authored one of the most incisive books about the Malvinas-Falklands conflict, responds:

> "On the one hand, this was an intensely psychological war. Serious newspapers acted pragmatically. As information enterprises, they clearly knew how the war would probably turn out, but they also thought that Argentina should play the game. On the other hand, the only source of information about the story was Britain. What

could they do? Call London? How could they verify those sources?" (Interviewed at the *Clarín* offices in Buenos Aires, 17 December 1990).

Retired Vice-Admiral Fernando Millia, director of the oldest Latin American publication about naval strategy, *El Boletín del Centro Naval*, held the office of Press Secretary for the Argentine Navy during the war. He gives his viewpoint about the *Superb* phenomenon:

"I have a very particular view about the *Superb* case. When NATO moved from a 'flexible response' strategy to one of 'assured destruction', the weapons needed to implement the strategy also changed. Submarines, which usually use short range torpedoes, had to have nuclear warheads. The *Superb* was supposedly at Gibraltar when its deployment to the South Atlantic was announced. One week it was in Scotland at a U.S. submarine base where nuclear warheads are kept! I suspect that the *Superb* went to change its conventional torpedoes for nuclear warheads, thus preparing for the eventual necessity of delivering a massive response in Argentine territory. The objective was the continent."

Do you believe that the submarine reached the waters off the Malvinas-Falklands?

"No, I don't think that she went farther than Ascension Island. The submarine's location was never pinpointed in technical terms, that is to say, with radar. An espionage operative told us that there were two submarines in the area. I think that British intelligence services promoted a certain idea to the media, but I have no reliable information. The European press had the information first and reports influenced each other. As in every war there were different versions of the story. In war, information is always foggy." (Interviewed 16 December 1990, in Buenos Aires)

Horacio Verbitsky, one of Argentina's most important opinion makers and editor-in-chief of the leftist *Pagina/12* newspaper, summarises the information strategy surrounding the *Superb* in the following manner:

"The *Superb* was an exceptional case. The whole incident was mostly about generating an Argentine psychological response. It was an imaginary war; it was never really planned to go to war. What was planned was a gigantic, psychological operation. The *Superb* episode, for example, resulted in the Argentine fleet being unable to operate comfortably because of fear or phantom submarines. The interesting thing about this psychological action is that it went against the very Argentines – the enemy that had to be confused was an internal one. Everything was used to dissimulate the facts. There was always the magical belief that things would take care of themselves." (Interviewed 18 December, 1990 in Buenos Aires)

In a research report about a New York City crime wave which had been covered by several New York papers, Fishman postulates that the press itself created the crime wave:

"I discovered something that made me wonder whether the entire news production process was creating the crime wave it was reporting. [...] As I checked with other journalists, I found that many had doubts about the reality of the crime wave. Still, no one could resist reporting it. The crime wave was a force which weighed heavily on their judgment of what constituted news, and it simply could not be ignored. Clearly, some kind of system was operating. Something in the news production process was creating the crime wave. What was it?" (Fishman 1980: 5)

The newspapers organised a frame of reference which converted a few news stories into an entire belief system. This internally nourished system was sufficiently stable to allow the story about the submarine to acquire a life of its own. In the media continuum, the story simply became a stabilised element in a flux of rumours.

Were, or weren't, British and Argentine submarines present in the area blockaded by the British? To answer this question we must turn to historical documentation and reconstruct, *a posteriori*, the entire interpretative circuit. Of course submarines were present in the area, but not the ones indicated by the press. Furthermore, their manoeuvres did not even take place on the dates stated by the press. The six submarines employed by the British Task Force were:

1. The *Spartan* and the *Splendid* from the Swiftsure class with a weight of 4,500 tons, a crew of 93 and a speed of 30 knots. Each carried five modified Tigerfish torpedoes and began operations on 12 April.
2. The *Conqueror*, the *Valiant* and the *Courageous* from the Churchill and Valiant class; each 4,500 tons, a crew of 103, and a speed of 30 knots. Equipped with six modified Tigerfish torpedoes, they commenced operations on 16 April, 16 May and 30 May

respectively.
3. The *Onyx* from the Oberon and Porpoise class; 2,410 tons, 69 crew members on board, a velocity of 12 knots and eight modified Tigerfish torpedoes. She started operations on the 28 May. (Hastings and Jenkins 1983: 374)

Up until 10 April, the press continued to construct and furnish a possible media world for the *Superb*. The *Spartan* and the *Splendid*, however, were the first British submarines to enter the operation zone, and they did not enter the zone prior to 12 April. Argentine submarines such as the *Salta* or the *Santa Fé* – highly damaged during the battle for the Georgia Islands at the end of April – waged intense attacks until the Argentine surface ship *General Belgrano* was sunk on 3 May by British forces. The reader, though, can only be apprised of this "extra media" information after the war from specialised British and Argentine publications.

Returning to the possible world, after 10 April, and above all after 12 April, two media information constructions melded together: one, the survival of the fictional story of the *Superb* in the PMW 1; the other, fictional and non-fictional information about the other submarines that made up the British expedition in PMW 2. From the point of view of the model media reader, the construction of news credibility appeared sound and the possibility of deontic ascription remained indeterminable.

The statements of unofficial textual sources from the Argentine Air Force and Navy were later revealed to be the closest to the actual truth. Despite their accuracy, however, they were unable to produce an information rupture that was sufficiently potent to recontextualise the frame of existing presuppositions which the model media reader had constructed over the passing days. No Argentine statement had the positional power to produce a communication catastrophe in the British strategy.

The rumour's evolution curve in relation to political and military events during the first month of the conflict indicates that the point of major information tension – or what can be called identifying property attributions – in the *Superb*'s possible world, occurred on 31 March, 1 and 2 April; moments before the landing of the rumour in Argentina and of the Argentines on the islands. Reports dedicated to the rumour on those dates averaged four a day. The rumour's second wind occurred during the time span between American Secretary of State Alexander Haig's London-Buenos Aires trip, with an average of three stories a day. The date 12 April 1982 is the epicentre of the maximum point of information tension about both the rumour and negotiation attempts; on this date *Clarín* simultaneously published PMW 1 and PMW 2.

What makes the *Superb* case especially interesting is that on 13 April, after Haig and the Military Junta's statements that diplomatic attempts to reach a negotiated solution had collapsed, and after the arrival of the *Spartan* and *Splendid* in the blockade zone, the *Superb* rumour was thrust into crisis. This crisis continued until the submarine's profile was totally eclipsed, thereby marking how the entire construction of the small world of the submarine formed part of the great world of strategy of the war. At this point the analyst, a "privileged" reader, in as much as having simultaneous access to textual and extra-textual evidence becomes another type of Model Reader, can test interpretative hypotheses and formulate a sufficiently cautious group of meta abductions:

1. On the one hand, the rumour, as has been accurately noted by Kapferer, always functions as a simplified explanation system through its provision of an organisational frame in which to place daily perceptions of events (Kapferer 1987: 80). In this sense, the rumour is viewed as a narrative not far from myth. The *Superb* story filled the first page of the first week of the conflict. The *Clarín* reader could hold onto a series of cognitive hypotheses which could easily be accepted in such a small – and easily manipulated – world.
2. On the other hand, the possible media world which circulated because of the rumour forced official textual sources from both countries to take a position about the accuracy of the reported information and about the accuracy of the entire communication interaction.

The *Superb* story demonstrates the inverted importance that unofficial textual sources have over official ones: unofficial sources, entering the information scene to confirm or deny the media-invented phenomena, exalted it to the status of "event" simply because it had been referred to by official sources. The entire information circuit is thus legitimised. The extant presuppositions of British and Argentine official textual sources act as a counter-legitimisation discourse. They become one more element in the construction of the *Superb*'s possible world. Viewed from this perspective, the *Superb* story is not very far from the genre of historical novel which intertwines historical persons with fictional ones in the same textual scenery.

It is very possible that British intelligence sources, who had to gain time until the actual arrival of the Task Force on the islands, created the rumour so that it would be picked up by the media. The media system, however, is the entity which effectively produced the rumour. Official British textual sources confirmed the story indirectly with a conglomerate of textual strategies which produced "false information" that acquires the status of "news report" the moment it is embraced by the press. While the British Navy was being deployed, these official sources were supposed to fill the time lag with an opportune story capable of capturing the reader with the same type of suspense present in a mystery novel. As such, the rumour had to have a carefully timed life span in order to be effective.

A construction of the rumour which categorises it as a kind of media verisimilitude placed the Argentine official and unofficial textual sources who espoused it in a position which is, at the very least, uncomfortable. Deprived of a meta-discursive strategy aimed at defusing the *Superb*'s possible media world, Argentine sources joined the rearguard of the British strategy. Although this posture gave the Argentines the opportunity of double-crossing the British strategy, they failed to sink the British communication plan. When British nuclear submarines truly began to operate in the area, the Argentine media opportunity had already passed. And the newspaper? *Clarín* established a double media pact with the reader: one, the constructed possible media world legitimisation and identification system, was internal to the media; the other, external to the reader, played with a fictional and factual double register. Everything that was publishable got published, without discrimination, just like the great book of the world.

The news information strategies failed to escape the logic of their own internal production system and their main loyalty – their Great Pact – is not so much to the readers as to themselves. Perhaps because of this, the antagonistic categories of telling the truth or lying – as John Searle would say – as they adhere to a particular extra-textual reference source, are not sufficiently operative inside a media world. In the dichotomy, the press creates, through its articulations – which are based on its own information sources – and through its production of possible worlds, such an effective form of unreality that it can step beyond the bounds of the actual events. This process confirms the way that the media legitimises itself and its version of factual events, i.e. media truth. What comes into play in the consumption of information discourse is not verification, but credibility.

Many Years Later

An analysis of the British role in the Malvinas-Falklands War by Lord Franks for the British Parliament, known as the Franks Report, was published on 18 January 1983. Article No. 331 states:

> In conclusion, we believe that action should have been taken during the first phase of the Georgia Islands crisis which was consistent to the deployment of ships in the sector. The opinion of Lord Carrington is that the use of surface ships would not have gone unnoticed and would have implied serious threat precisely at the time that the government sought to avoid any action which might cause provocation. An intervention could have caused a series of attacks by the Argentines against the Falkland islands, in the face of which the government would have been forced to respond. This objection is not the same as that to the deployment of a submarine, because the possibility existed of obscuring her movements. The decision to deploy the first nuclear submarine was taken on Monday, March 29th, 1982." (*Falkland Islands Review: Report of a Committee of Privy Counsellors. Chmn. Lord Franks (Command 8787)* 1983: 235).

Lord Franks's report raises a final question: Was a secret submarine deployed on 29 March, hidden from radar and from the media who were focused on describing the *Superb*? Was the *Superb* a dupe, a British intelligence strategy, meant to obscure the existence of the "real" submarine which was deployed on the 29 March and whose identity and qualities remain unknown? To date, the question is unanswered, but does point to the vertigo created by information disseminated during conflicts: A wants B to believe that C, and so on to infinity.

ACTS OF WAR

Information from the Front
The construction of the *Superb* submarine's possible world, and its circulation in the Argentine press, served as a British information strategy: it was a dissuasive rumour during the preparation of the war's first military offensive, i.e. the British landing on the Southern Georgia Islands on 25 April 1982. The Parroquet Operation, as the British recuperation of the islands was called, has been amply reconstructed by British and Argentine historical sources, neither of which differ in their evaluation of the events (Hastings and Jenkins 1983: 143 ff.; Moro 1985:148). This episode, which stood out for both British and Argentines more for its political value than its strategic one, allows analysis of the first case of a large scale Argentine military misinformation effort in the national press. It also highlights *Clarín*'s and *La Nación*'s strategies in diffusing military communiqués from official sources and information from the papers' own sources, neither of which always coincided. Censorship and auto-censorship, the decision to inform, and the production of fiction became intertwined in the press. As a constant in war information, rumours about the *Superb* submarine continued in a news wave, this time of Argentine military sources, that constructed the newspapers' agendas from the last days of April to the middle of May.

The British ice-breaker *Endurance,* its destroyers *Plymouth* and *Antrim* and the frigate *Brilliant*, all essential elements of the British Task Force which had initiated the naval blockade of the islands on 12 April, sailed from Ascension Island to the Georgias. From 21 May on, they carried out their first manoeuvres in extremely poor weather conditions. These British ships reached the Georgias on 24 April. A real Argentine submarine, the ARA *Santa Fe*, which had been in service since WWII, could be found in the Cumberlands Bahia being fitted. All historians concur in finding it surprising that, after a strong military attack by the British, this submarine managed to stay afloat and to reach Grytviken. Sailor Alberto Macias was injured and Captain Juan Lagos successfully evacuated the contingent on board. After the intensive bombing of the ARA *Santa Fe* and other Argentine positions launched at 14:45 local time, Mayor Sheridan's command advanced with 150 British troops. The Argentine guard, which also had approximately 140 soldiers and was commanded by Captain Alfredo Astiz formally surrendered at 17:15 local time. The act of surrender was signed on the 26 April on the icebreaker *Endurance* and noted that the surrender of these men was unconditional.

Acts of War

Already a prisoner of the British, Argentine Navy officer Felix Artuso, son and grandson of marines, who had been on the ARA *Santa Fe*, took on the desperate and individual act of attempting to sabotage the British submarine *Conqueror*. Shot by a British sailor patrolling the area, he was buried by the British with military honours and was the only victim of the Parraquet Operation.[1]

The case of the information cover-up of the events on the Georgias reveals an extremely illustrative discursive interplay in the relationships between typical censorship and self-censorship mechanisms during conflicts. In addition to this, it is an example of how British and Argentine information sources were used and thereby implicated in a secondary polemic about the construction of media truth.

The first news stories about possible incidents in the Georgias appeared simultaneously on 24 April in *Clarín, La Nación* and *La Prensa*:

Clarín: "British ships 90 kilometres from the Georgias.
La Nación: "British ships in attack position. Two ships face the Georgias."
La Prensa: "The British fleet in the area surrounding the islands. Advancing on a heavy sea in two groups which are directed at the Malvinas and the Georgias."

The treatment of the story by the part of the three papers' headlines differs in this first presentation to the reader: mitigated in *La Prensa*'s version (in the area surrounding), evaluative in *La Nación*'s (in attack position), and impersonal in *Clarín*'s (British ships). The media world that is beginning to be delineated has a sole empirical source here: Italy's ANSA press agency. The agency affirms that the British fleet has been divided at the 40th parallel and is advancing toward the Georgias. *La Prensa* adds that the British fleet is entering a zone in range of Argentine planes. There is no reference to military information.

On 25 April, when the Argentine sailors had already surrendered, *Clarín* produces its first temporal and spatial disjunction, affirming on its first page that "British ships remain in an area close to the Southern Georgias in the middle of a storm." The item, which comes from an Argentine military source, informs that two war ships are in the

---

[1] For the political importance and reconstruction of the battle for the Georgias, the Argentine rendition, and the death of Artuso, cf. Adams 1986: 80-84; Verbitsky 1984: 157-68; Hastings and Jenkins 1983: 115, 143-51; Cardoso *et al.* 1983: 202; Ruiz Moreno 1989: 31; Moro 1985: 148-52.

immediate area, but that "any attack on the Georgias cannot be realistically carried out before Tuesday, the 27th". The Argentine agency, DYN, adds that Argentine ships are maintaining "total control of the situation", but that their position is a "military secret".

From this information, the newspapers constructed two possible worlds that were alternative to each other, but not inter-changeable. One, from a military source, had the Argentine forces in the islands continuing to resist for over ten days with no sign of surrender. The other, from a British source, had the Argentines surrender at 17:15 hours on 25 April. Between the construction of these two antagonistic worlds, *Clarín* tried independently to play the strategy of its own space, which was identified with the reader's space, until it could no longer sustain the Argentine military's possible world and finally chose the British one. In reality, what *Clarín* carried out was the construction of a multiple Model Reader. This time, it was respectful of the worlds it put into circulation and took care that they never collided with each other. The reader thus remained free to choose one or the other version of the story.

In effect, it was in the paper's inner pages that the reader learned the British source's information: after two hours of fighting, the Argentines surrendered. Defence Minister John Nott announced this event in a live radio and television message at the precise moment that Prime Minister Thatcher was announcing it to the Queen.

In *Clarín,* the reader finds the official British version which notes that "Argentine troops offered only limited resistance to British forces and, at 18 hours England, time a white flag was hoisted over the Argentine position". The newspaper's headline is suggestive because it marks the distance between the media, the official textual source, and the reader: "The British government affirms that it is occupying the Georgia Islands".

Valerie Adams analyses the behaviour of the British press in the Georgias:

> The South Georgia incident provides an interesting case history. [...] the attack on the submarine *Santa Fe* on Sunday, 25 April, was announced by late Monday morning. Thereafter, the retaking of South Georgia was widely reported, with supposedly detailed accounts of how it had been achieved – not always very accurate ones. Given the official reticence, inaccuracies are hardly surprising, since reporters had to rely largely on leaks and imagination. (Adams 1986: 81)

Acts of War

Argentine military stories

The following day, 26 April, communiqués began to be given out by official Argentine military sources. *Clarín* simultaneously published the Argentine and British military information. It is interesting to observe that the construction of the possible media world of the British landing is an implicit event that is never confirmed. The information is gradated drop by drop because, in principle, the Model Reader of this world cannot tolerate direct exposure to the events.

In communiqué no. 30, the Military Junta highlights the "elevated morale and fighting ability" of the Argentine troops, by which the British operation's success is becoming increasingly difficult. In no. 31, it affirms that Argentine forces had been "reduced", but were resisting with "unbroken spirit". After this, communication was cut with the islands and the Argentine commandos broke off their own codes.

In communiqué no. 32, given on Monday 26 April at 00.50 hours, we find:

> For tactical reasons, communications have been cut with the naval forces defending the Georgia islands. The apparent initial triumph of the British forces owes itself to the notable numerical superiority of its troops, but does not, mean that they exercise unrestricted control of the islands. Our forces are holding their initial positions and continue to fight on land with an unbroken spirit of combat based on the moral superiority of he who defends his homeland's territory. Independent of the final result of this difficult battle, the basic objectives fixed by the Military Junta in terms of the recuperation of the islands will remain constant and will expressly rest on the fact that sovereignty will not be negotiated, nor will national dignity be placed into risk at any price. (*Clarín*, 26 April, "The Military Junta informs about the British attack")

According to Argentine journalist Oscar Raúl Cardoso:

> The truth of the matter was, as it so often was during those days, information that the rhetoric of official communiqués didn't even touch. Communiqué no. 31 assured that the naval officer (Astiz) had decided to "break his codes" and his radio equipment – thereby voluntarily isolating his troops – before beginning to resist the British. In actuality, less than two hours after the beginning of the British attack, Astiz order that the white flag be waved next to the Argentine one and proceeded to surrender the plaza, without having barely resisted. (Cardoso *et al.* 1983, 202)

What strategy does *Clarín* use to publish its story of this first Argentine defeat? In first place, it frees its own sources from responsibility: it is the Military Junta which is informing. The paper alerts the reader to this under the suggestive title "Surprise and serenity", with which it should remain very clear that only the Military Junta « has and expresses information referring to military actions registered in the islands of the Southern Atlantic" (*Clarín,* 26 April, "Surprise and serenity", Carlos Marcelo Thiery, special correspondent on the Comodoro Rivadavia).

The Model Reader sketched out by *Clarín* differs from the military world. The reader is freed to make his or her own inferences and to reach his or her own conclusion by simply comparing the register of the news presented by the paper. At no time does *Clarín* enter into the media world designed by the two opposing combatants. Because the newspaper is obliged, however, to respect the rules of news control handed down by the government, *Clarín* titles its front page of 26 April "The British invasion is being resisted in the Georgias", but in its inner pages, based on one of its own sources, it announces that the Argentines surrendered after two hours of combat.

As we have seen, the construction of a news flux operates by the successive selection and accumulation of elements. The media news story, in its elaboration of verisimilitudes, condenses the details. The news story progressively fills the newspaper's agenda with new elements in a continuous chain.

Finally, in a report entitled "It wasn't a surprise", by one of the newspaper's own sources, we are informed that Argentine intelligence services had pointed out that the Georgias would be the first British objective. On page four, and under the title "The Junta informs about the British attack", communiqués 27, 28, 29, and 30 are published without additional comment, thereby giving the impression that the paper is trying to distance itself from the military's information.

Journalist Ricardo Kirschbaum explains *Clarín*'s treatment of these Argentine military information sources during this first phase of the war:

> "We couldn't counteract the Argentine military's information. There were communiqués that we could not validate. We had diplomatic sources and this was the most truthful information we had because it was independent of the military strategy. We discovered that we knew very little about what was happening. We didn't have the whole story." (Interviewed 17 December 1992, in Buenos Aires).

On 26 April, *La Prensa* gave information about the British attack under the heading, "British forces land on the Georgia Islands". The report noted that British forces landed after tenacious resistance by Argentine troops and repeated *Clarín*'s information as having come from one of its own sources. It mixed in the construction of the military's possible media world and reported that, after a "self-sacrificing resistance", the reduced Argentine force had decided to destroy their communication codes and fight to the last man. *La Prensa* also bent to the double information strategy by publishing a second title on its first page, and citing the information as having come from London: "Announcement of re-capture in London."[2]

For its part, *La Nación* highlighted the British invasion of the Georgias, emphasising in its version, by one of its own sources, that the British attack began with the bombing of the Argentine submarine the ARA *Santa Fe* and that retreating Argentine troops had blown up the submarine themselves. The newspaper's version respects its initial strategy: the information is "deferred" by the mediation of the paper and is presented in the context of Chancellor Costa Méndez's negotiations in Washington.

The construction of the possible Argentine military world appears in an indirect style: "The Argentine military high command has communicated in an emphatic manner that, whatever the result of the battle to liberate the Georgias, in no way will it affect Argentina's position in the Malvinas." *La Nación*, however, gives the British landing as fact and titles its 26 April edition with "British invasion of the Georgias". In another article on the same date, this paper publishes a story by AP in which Argentine troops have surrendered after twenty-five British troops disembarked on the islands. Here, the headline strategy follows the self-censorship principle and *La Nación* entitles the story, "Tenacious resistance in the Southern Georgias".

Bartolomé Mitre, then owner and director of *La Nación*, explains the press's delicate situation in its use of military information sources under censorship:

> The circumstances showed that the source of events in the theatre of operations – land, sea and air warfare – implied censorship. It should be noted that, from a news point of view, they were uniform in their conditions for everyone, except for the government's own

---

[2] To follow the nationalist position of the newspaper *La Prensa*, see a book by one of its editors (Schoenfeld 1982).

press and information agencies. With a more or less critical sense of the conflict's development and details, we can see that the media supported the rights of Argentina to the islands. (Written response by Bartolomé Mitre, Buenos Aires, 17 December 1990)

Just Who Are *Los Lagartos?*: The Fictional Micro-Story

How could the military power structure support the story of Argentine resistance when the independent media had chosen the strategy of publishing the two-fold register of information from official British and official Argentine sources, both of which radically contradicted each other? What the military discourse did was to construct a micro-story within the already delineated possible media world. In this micro-story, a Navy commando group, *Los Lagartos* [The Lizards], under the direction of Captain Astiz, continued to resist.

This construction is interesting because it takes elements from possible media world (1), "The Battle of the Georgias", which began on 26 April, and in which a real captain named Astiz actually existed, and inserts him into another possible media world (2), "Resistance in the Georgias", as a credibility index. Elements were annulled that could enter into possible media world (2), such as an Argentine surrender, thereby establishing a causal continuity sustained by the theme of the narrative. This is a double fictionalisation operation, in which elements of the two possible media worlds reciprocally support and legitimise each other.

In taking the media as a support, however, i.e. as a heterogeneous and polyphonic support, fictionalisation enters into collusion with other narratives that are simultaneously circulating. The world of literary fiction is closed onto itself, even though it may be "open" in its interpretations. The world of the media, however, is open in terms of the circulation of narratives, but is "closed" in terms of the type of media contract that it attempts to establish.

While waiting for the surrender to be confirmed by an Argentine military source, the reader finds on the front page of *Clarín*'s 27 April edition, "The Military Junta announces that naval troops are maintaining their position in the Georgias". In effect, official communiqué no. 33 denies the British report of a supposed surrender, but it does affirm that "elements of the Armada continue to resist".

For its part, *La Prensa* gives out a military source report according to which Special Forces are fighting in Leith. A highly placed navy officer "gave strategic details" of the actions being taken in the South, in which the eventual loss of the islands forms a "calculated risk" for Argentina's Armed Forces (*La Prensa,* 27 April, "The Military Junta denies reports about the Georgia Islands"). But, thanks to the circulation of narratives, in another section of the same newspaper, reporter Jesús Iglesias Rouco reports that the islands are now occupied by the British and lets the imminent attack of the Malvinas-Falklands be inferred (*La Prensa*, 27 April, "Two offensives").

On 28 April, *Clarín* maintains its strategy of simultaneously publishing British and Argentine military source information and, for the first time, presents the actors from this hypothetical resistance. *Clarín* always notes that it is Argentine military sources who are confirming and the paper takes pains to separate itself from this textual source. In the headline "They confirm the resistance of commandos in the Georgias", it is the military possible media world that confirms the presence of Argentine Navy commandos known as *Los Lagartos,* trained for high-risk operations, who are resisting British troops and, most importantly of all, whose battle is not yet over. The unidentified source does admit that British troops "have recuperated the islands' capital and port", but states that this was "a calculated risk", and finally affirms that the operation was an Argentine victory because "the action blocked the British before they were able to attempt a recapture of the Malvinas". In the controversy, one of the British Defence Ministry's spokesmen, Derek Knight, states on the same day that no combat is presently underway in the Georgias (*Clarín,* 28 April, "They confirm the resistance of commandos in the Georgias").

The position of official Argentine textual sources in this episode of surrender in the Georgias was that it was a calculated risk. The Model Reader can be comforted in knowing that everything is under control, just as it was in the statements of unofficial Argentine sources about the *Superb*. The most important thing is always to keep the Model Reader calm. In reality, though, this enunciative position was made possible through the stubborn defence of the possible media world that had been constructed by military communiqués. In effect, four days after the Argentine surrender on 25 April, Brigadier Major José Miret, Secretary of the Military Junta's strategic office, states in Washington, before reporter María Luisa Avignolo of the news magazine *Gente y la Actualidad*:

> *Is the occupation of the islands a defeat for Argentina?*
> "Not at all. It had been foreseen that the Georgias, which were the most likely islands for the British to carry out their first attack, were those that we had the least possibility of defending. But the battle of the Georgias gave evidence to the courage of our soldiers who resisted and who, today, Tuesday, continue to resist."

> *Does the military government accept continuing negotiations with England in this situation?*
>
> "In this situation the country cannot accept continuing to negotiate because the rules of the game have not been respected. Furthermore, the British do not inspire confidence, and have not done so as of the moment they attacked while negotiations were under-way." (*Gente y La Actualidad*, no. 875, 29 April, 16-18, "Two Argentine officers speak", interview by reporter María Luisa Avignolo)[3]

Meanwhile, in its attempt to gloss over the loss of the islands, *La Nación* publishes an extensive report about the Argentine Navy's position. Here we find the function of constructing "tempered unreality" in the media, which was characteristic of the official Argentine information position:

> In naval circles last night, statements were made that began to dissipate doubts. Psychological warfare by Great Britain was attributed as being the root of doubts about the status of the battle in the Georgia Islands, islands which are being defended by a small number of Naval forces. [...] Naval sources consider that "the fallacy" of official British communiqués is being placed in evidence as the hours pass and as that which is actually occurring in the theatre of operations is coming to light. [...] Parallel to, and through different channels, information was learned which included elements considered to be based in fact. This information indicated the losses being experienced by the invaders and the still ongoing resistance of a group of our forces. (*La Nación*, 28 April, "The following hours are considered to be decisive ones")

Argentinian historian Rubén Moro analysed the effect that the *Lagartos*' episode had on Argentine troops:

> Meanwhile, in Buenos Aires, the news media were filled with stories whose origin was purposely unclear, in which our troops were supposedly resisting in the style of *guerrilla* warfare. Short-wave radio communications of unknown origin reported on the supposed British losses caused by the Lagartos. [...] Once the truth became

---

[3] On the behaviour of *Gente* and its support of the military report about the *Lagartos*, see Verbitsky 1984: 157-68.

clear, this "psychological action" produced a high amount of demoralisation among the troops, and added the punch of lowering Argentine public opinion about its Armed Forces. This effect was felt not only during the conflict, but much afterwards as well. This fable, nourished by some of the news media in the capital, and not duly denied by official organisms, took root even in the three members of the Military Junta, who believed it to be true up to the return of the prisoners from San Pedro Island. (Moro 1985: 152)

On 29 April, Argentine military sources were insistent about the resistance micro-story. They affirmed that one hundred sharp shooters were holding off British troops (*Clarín,* 29 April, "Military actions to occur in the upcoming hours"). In this case of censorship and self-censorship, what is certain is that no Argentine newspaper ever reported, via its own sources, about the Argentine surrender in the *Georgias*. The event was always presented as coming exclusively from British press sources. The "small world" about the British invasion ceased to appear in the press as of 29 April, when a third wave of information began. This wave dealt with an imminent attack on the Malvinas.

Meanwhile, up until 6 May, news magazine *Gente y la Actualidad* continues its report of the *Lagartos*' resistance in the Georgias:

> Today, more than ten days have passed without cease in the battle which battle continues in the Georgia Islands, a battle that has been somewhat forgotten since the British attack on the Malvinas. [...] The battle is still going on in the Georgias. Fifty Argentines are taking on the British army. (*Gente y la Actualidad*, no. 876, 6 May, "The pilot who flew over the Georgias speaks", by Gabriela Cociffi)

What To Do with those Cumbersome Prisoners of War

Without any concern for the possible media world's development, Argentine forces, comprised of approximately 150 naval personnel under the command of Captain Alfredo Astiz, were taken prisoner on 25 April.[4] The implicit report about the surrender – and its denial – became concrete in headlines as of 13 May, the date of the Argentine prisoners' arrival from the Georgias:

---

[4] See also the version by Gamba 1984.

13 May
> *Clarín*: "The Georgias: prisoners arrive in Montevideo".

14 May
> *Clarín*: "The return today of civilians and military personnel from the Georgias".
> *La Nación*: "Freed prisoners arrive today from the Georgias. They are 150 Argentine military personnel and 39 civilians taken prisoner by British forces nineteen days ago."
> *La Prensa*: "Civilians and military personnel taken captive in the Georgias arrive today."

15 May
> *Clarín*: "189 Argentines captured in the Georgias have returned."
> *La Nación*: "189 ex-prisoners from the Georgias arrived yesterday in Buenos Aires."
> *La Prensa*: "The return of personnel from the Georgias. An emotional reception given to the civilians and military men repatriated by the Red Cross."

The differences in the treatment of these headlines mark a final textual element which frames the report as ascribable to a possible media world. While *La Nación* constantly qualifies them as "prisoners", thus reminding the reader of the amount of time passed, *Clarín* and *La Prensa* fluctuate in their use of "prisoners" and "captives". The "return of personnel" in *La Prensa* and the "return today of civilians and military men" in *Clarín* confuses the status of those Argentines in the media memory: they may have come back because they had fought, but not necessarily because they were prisoners.

On 14 May, in a report signed by special envoy Arnaldo Paganetti, "A Long Captivity", the reader learns that the prisoners were handed over to the Argentine Embassy in Montevideo without the presence of reporters and that "Argentine authorities wanted to quickly resolve this problem without any type of propaganda". It is only in *Clarín*'s 15 May issue, 21 days after the fact, that it is possible to learn that the men were captured on "25 April". While the ex-prisoners express themselves about the weeks of captivity, Captain Hugo Bicain declares to the press that "we will recuperate the Georgias". The last report from a military Argentine source about the episode in the Georgia Islands is communiqué no. 45: "Headquarters wishes to communicate that the personnel which intervened in the actions on the Southern Georgia Islands will arrive in Buenos Aires on May 14th."

Oscar Raúl Cardoso frames this military information strategy as an attempt to establish a hegemonic account of the events.

"There were orders, but I don't remember having received specific orders from the government. There were daily meetings with government spokesmen. Opinions were given and the press took them up as information. Actually, it was a hegemonic account of reality. Frankly, it still is not clear to me if this press cover-up was done in order to lie or to tell the truth. In my own case, I always checked sources, except for those which came from outside Argentina and which were generally trustworthy. But information was always checked, including cable information, which was always compared with cables from other agencies.

"I think that in the Malvinas conflict the official account entered into crisis – just as the account about the concentration camps did in the 'dirty war' – and this period didn't leave better newspaper products in its wake. All of us participated in the same hegemonic account and we all paid for it in terms of credibility." (Interview with Oscar Raúl Cardoso, Buenos Aires, 17 December 1990)

A Very Special Prisoner: The Case of Alfredo Astiz

As of 15 May, and through the EFE, AFP and AP agencies, information suddenly appeared stating that Alfredo Astiz, Navy officer in the Georgia Islands, had not been repatriated by the Red Cross, but remained prisoner on Ascension Island in order to be interrogated by the British for human rights violations. The governments of France and Switzerland accused him of crimes against two French nuns and a young Swiss woman (*Clarín,* 17 May, AFP, AP "Problems for the Red Cross; *Clarín,* 17 May, EFE, "Prisoner"; *La Nación,* 21 May, TELAM, "Captain Astiz's situation"; *Clarín,* 21 May, TELAM, "The situation of Captain Astiz").

Clarín again presents developing reports from international agency sources. It finally picks up the version of the story by the official Argentine agency, TELAM, but reports it in an indirect style:

> The official agency TELAM informed that the British government is holding Captain Alfredo Astiz as a "prisoner of war" In the last few days, the governments of France and Switzerland have made formal requests that Captain Astiz be interrogated about supposed events which took place in Argentina during the time of the fight against subversion in that country.

And so, Vice Admiral (RE) Fernando Millia admits that the story of the resistance of the *Lagartos* commandos and their captain, Astiz, was an Argentine Navy counter-information strategy:

"The only case I am aware of in which a distortion of facts was produced by a member of the Armada was the episode concerning the *Lagartos* commando. A troop of special commandos was invented, among which figured officer Astiz, who put up a resistance in the Georgia Islands. The press reported on the heroic resistance of the group. This was not true and the group as such never existed. This was a classic case of attempting to counter and cover-up enemy information, but it later underwent an unexpected deviation at the moment when the islands were surrendered and Astiz was on them." (Interview with Vice Admiral (RE) Fernando Millia, Buenos Aires, 16 December 1990)

In another interview for this book, Horacio Verbitsky noted how the force of the media account reached up to the high command of the Armada:

"It was basically information that was directed and centralised by the State. It reproduced the information model that had been used during the 'dirty war': communiqué plus leaks plus dramatisation of human interest stories. One shouldn't forget that in the case of the disappeared the use of information sources began to escape the control of military and the first reports about the 'dirty war' came to us from those outside the country.

"What I found and noted in my book about news-magazine *Gente y la Actualidad*'s behaviour was to what point it was all a duplicitous process. The case of the élite *Lagartos* commandos is a good example of this. Admiral Anaya confessed in statements after the war that he had believed that the *Lagartos* existed and that they weren't invented by the Navy! Another example is the attack on the air-carrier Hermes, where there were supposedly dead who actually never died. There a thousand of such cases. The sources that we had were always the same: official information plus leaks." (Interview with Horacio Verbitsky, Buenos Aires, 18 December, 1990)

It is worth citing the statements of Admiral Jorge Isaac Anaya, member of the Military High Command during the war, while being judged by the Commission on the Analysis and Evaluation for Responsibility in the Conflict of the Southern Atlantic, also known as the Rattenbach Commission:

"I had come to believe that there was a full-scale battle going on in the Georgias, and it wasn't until later that I learned that the whole thing had been staged by the Navy. [...] I was convinced that bloody battles were going on in the Georgias because of the news that was in the press. Since I had no communication with the Georgias, I was shocked when I learned that our forces were all prisoners at the same time that I was reading in the papers about the *Lagartos* attacking here and the *Lagartos* attacking there. I had been duped." (Quoted by Verbitsky 1984: 167-8)

This is an excellent case of a Model Reader of the possible military media world and of the credibility effect.

STORIES, SINKINGS AND TORPEDOES

The War Chronicle
As of 8:00 am, 30 April, the British blockade around 2000 miles of the Southern Atlantic had been achieved. The Argentine Military Junta responded with communiqué no. 37, in which it stated that it considered as hostile all British ships and planes to be found in the area (*Clarín*, 3 April0, "The Southern Atlantic is a war zone").[1] The BBC had already reported that British forces had three options before them: establishing a beach head, establishing an air-naval blockade, or attempting an immediate assault on the islands. For its part, US newspaper *The Washington Post* leaked that the landing of British commandos was certain, while CBS news supported this report, affirming that a hundred frogmen would soon land (Adams 1986: 87).

For some authors, the war – which had never been technically declared – began on 1 May with the attack of British Sea Harrier planes on installations at Puerto Argentino. The operation was known as the "Black Bud Raid" (Adams 1986: 84; Ruiz Moreno 1986: 72ff.; Gavshon and Rice 1984: 107ff.; Hastings and Jenkins 1983: 164ff.) The first official Argentine report in the press about the event took place at 8am on both official radio and television stations, with the reading of military communiqué no. 38, in which the Military Junta informed of the British attack. Next, the Secretary of Public Information, Rodolfo Baltiérrez, made a statement about successive meetings with the Military Committee. As of that moment, only Military Headquarters – and not the Military Junta – centralised information about successive attacks and new communiqués began to represent official military source information (*Clarín*, 2 May, "Official communiqués").

Clarín presented the information on the front page of its 2 May edition, stating that at 4:40 local time, 1 May, British Harrier planes attacked the airfield at Puerto Argentino. One of the newspaper's own sources reported that Argentine anti-air defence managed to hit two planes and attack British ships. As it had already done with the British landing in the Georgias, *Clarín* took pains to distance itself from official military source information and noted that "The development of these actions is known through successive official communiqués and through the report of an envoy from the official press agency, TELAM, which is the only press unit authorised in the Malvinas" (*Clarín*, 2 May, "Heavy

---

[1] TIAR resolution of 26 April 1982. See, among others, Gamba 1984: 163; Moro 1985: 116.

fighting in the Malvinas").

A witness of the attack, Commodore Hugo Maiorano, stated:

"On May 1st there was a large air attack on the base by Sea Harriers. One of these planes swooped down and shot at a Púcara plane that was taking off. Eight officers were on it. A bomb hit the plane, it burst into flames, and Lieutenant Jukic died. The press later invented a different story and had him killed while attacking the British aircraft carrier *Hermes*, which is something that never happened. The British attacked close to the airstrip. Our anti-air weapons could destroy low-flying planes, but not those above six thousand meters. After the 1st of May the British realized that it was too difficult to destroy the airstrip if they flew low and they changed their strategy so as to attack from over a height of six thousand meters. For this reason they never managed to destroy the base. We resisted throughout the whole conflict and I was taken prisoner on the 16th of June." (Interview with Commodore Hugo Maiorano on 11 January 1991, in Rosario)

Commodore Hugo Maiorano was a member of the Argentine Air Force High Command and the officer in charge of anti-air artillery defence in Puerto Argentino (formerly Port Stanley). Maiorano's account coincides with Gavshon and Rice's finding that the 1 May attack on Puerto Argentino, in which 21 bombs were dropped on its airstrip, began a British military escalation despite the diplomatic negotiations begun by Alexander Haig and then carried out by Fernando Belaunde Terry (Gavshon and Rice 1984: 104).

None of the Argentine newspapers analysed here reported the death of Lieutenant Jukic on 1 May. Neither did official communiqués which, furthermore, failed to note the eight casualties reported in Captain Pablo Carballo's interview, "God and the Falcons", for *Siete Dias* magazine (Buenos Aires, 30 March 1983). *La Nación* reported: "Official information, diffused repeatedly by radio and television about military actions, do not note human casualties" (*La Nación*, 2 May, "British attacks on the Malvinas Islands were pushed off").

The report that Commodore Maiorano refers to about Argentine planes which, under the command of Lieutenant Jukic, damaged the *Hermes,* appears for the first time in *La Nación*'s 4 May issue, "A Púcara managed to damage the Hermes", using the DYN and TELAM as sources. *Gente y la Actualidad* then reported it in issue no. 876 on 6 May ("And the *Hermes* was too small") as well as in issue no. 878 on 20 May ("What's happening with the *Hermes*?"); and finally in issue no. 879 on

27 May ("Alejandro Jukic speaks: This was my brother, the man who attacked the Hermes"). Jukic's family did not make any counter-statements, denials, or press charges against any Argentine paper.

These first attacks, which were kept at bay by Argentine forces, highlight the theatre of the war and push aside other news because of their gravity. A third wave of information begins here, one that would continue through the middle of May, and which coincided with the definitive withdrawal of the British landing in the Georgias from the newspapers' agendas. The third wave sketched out a space that was strongly monopolised by bellicose actions. The newspapers, despite maintaining their enunciative strategies, globally developed a war chronicle that transformed the information discourse into a veritable epic narrative.

The British version of the attack was extremely confusing:

> The *Vulcan* raid on Stanley Airport finally took place early on the morning of May 1st. The initial Monday announcement of the raid was prompt, but cryptic, so that initially the media suggested that the attack and been carried out by *Harriers*. The British news cover-up initially hid the failure of the "Black Bud Raid": The British daily press of 3 May gave considerable coverage to the story, and all the papers followed the line in official announcements that the raid had been a success. Most gave detailed descriptions, presumably largely imaginary, of how it had been carried out. No one questioned the necessity for, or the value of, the operation. (Adams 1986: 87)

Analysing the triumphalism of the British press during the period, researchers from the Glasgow University Media Group (1985) demonstrated that Argentine information about the Black Bud Raid had been correct:

> Journalists found it difficult to admit that they had made mistakes [...]; it is clear that the raids were less successful than the authorities had reported [...]; it appeared as if some broadcasters had difficulty in saying that the Argentines could be telling the truth and the Ministry could be misinforming them [...]; the press in general embraced an interpretation that emphasised the successful execution of the operation.

Hanrahan and Fox note that the Argentine and British accounts of the events on the 1 May varied so greatly that it was impossible even to compare them. Twenty British Harriers were in involved in the operation. The Argentines held that they shot down two of them, but the British maintained that there were no losses (Hanrahan and Fox 1982: 10).

The Sinking of the ARA *General Belgrano*
On 30 April, three Argentine ships were detected on the radar of the *Conqueror*, the British nuclear submarine. On 1 May, its captain, Chris Wreford-Brown, informed his superiors that he had located the ARA *General Belgrano*, which had a crew of 1,042 men, and two Argentine destroyers, the *Bouchard* and the *Piedrabuena*. The *General Belgrano* was not outfitted with either anti-submarine devices or sonar. During thirty hours, while she sailed over 70 kilometres into the area blockaded by the British, the *Conqueror* silently followed her and waited to receive authorisation to attack. At the moment the order came, the peace plan of Peruvian president Fernando Belaunde Terry was being negotiated between Great Britain and Argentina.

On Sunday, 2 May, Sir Laurence Lewin, Admiral of the British Fleet, arrived at the British Prime Minister's Cabinet meeting, and requested authorisation to sink the *General Belgrano*, now found to the southeast of the blockaded area. At 14:00 local time, and before negotiations with Belaunde Terry had finished, the British Cabinet gave permission to attack. At 15:57 local time, the *Conqueror*'s captain ordered three torpedoes to be fired, two of which were direct hits. At 16:22 hours, the Argentine ship was already going down. Her captain, Hugo Bonzo, managed to evacuate 770 men in the following half-hour. At 17:01, the ARA *General Belgrano* had sunk. The survivors were rescued a day later. For its part, the *Conqueror* earned the distinction of being the first British nuclear submarine to sink an enemy ship since the Second World War (Hastings and Jenkins 1983: 168-72; Gavshon and Rice 1984: 129-40; Cardoso *et al.* 1983: 221-40; Moro 1985: 199-225).

On 3 May, *Clarín* published, on page 4, a General Headquarters report that "An Argentine ship has been attacked outside the blockade zone". The report simply stated that a British submarine had attacked the ARA *General Belgrano* to the southeast of the State Islands. On the same date, *La Nación* stated that, at 00:50 hours, General Headquarters had issued communiqué no. 15, in which the attack of the *General Belgrano* was reported. Initially the event is presented as the ship being "damaged" and *La Nación* tries to contextualise the report by separating itself from the military sources so designating it. Since this is the first information that exists about the attack on the ship, it is interesting to see how the newspaper gave official textual sources the role of narrators:

At 00:50 hours today, General Headquarters issued communiqué no. 15 in which it informs of the attack suffered by the cruiser *General Belgrano* as she sailed outside of the zone of maritime exclusion. The communiqué was given in the press room of the Government House by the Secretary of Public Information, Rodolfo Baltiérrez, who remained in that room until the information was transmitted over several local radio stations. General Headquarters' report constitutes the only official communication emitted yesterday about bellicose actions. It was preceded by contradictory versions of the report. The confirmation of the event established that the damage suffered by the ship was caused by a torpedo, and that other naval vessels had arrived to assist it. (*La Nación*, 3 May, "Attack by a British submarine")

La Nación presents all the information as coming from an official military source, thereby taking care specifically to establish who its enunciators are.[2] Immediately after, it will re-publish the report as having come from one of its own sources, and successive military communiqués will be used to complete and rectify the story as new details about the tragic sinking are known.

For its part, the Argentine Chancery confirms the sinking at 21:45 hours on 2 May. The event is first framed as an "attack" situated "outside of the blockade zone". From the first moment, the high number of survivors is highlighted. On 4 May, the story jumps to first page in the Argentine papers. *Clarín* entitles the report, "Shipwrecked sailors are rescued from the sunken cruiser. Argentina denounces the attack as having occurred outside of the war zone". It thus calls on a media pre-construction formed over the preceding days. In its inner pages, it publishes communiqué no. 16, in which we are told that "an attack by a British submarine indicates the sinking of the ship".

In its first page article, *La Nación*, working from one of its own sources, presents "a tragic testimony to the gravity the war is assuming"

---

[2] All Argentine military communiqués of the period were published in their entirety in *La Nación*. Below is the complete communiqué about the event: "The Government of the Argentine Republic, following the information given by GH today in communiqué no. 15, wishes to inform that: at 17:00 hours, on May 2nd, the cruiser, *ARA General Belgrano,* was attacked and sunk by a British submarine at a location situated at a southern latitude of 55 degrees and 24 minutes and a western longitude of 61 degrees and 32 minutes. The ship has a crew of 1042 men. Survivor rescue operations are being carried out" (*La Nación*, 4 May, "An evil act of armed aggression").

(*La Nación*, 4 May, "The cruiser *General Belgrano* was sunk outside of the blockade zone"). *La Prensa*, one day later, repeats the information contained in communiqué no. 16 in its article, "We confirm the sinking of the cruiser *ARA General Belgrano*". Official British confirmation of the sinking is given at the United Nations and dispatched through Reuters press agency (*Clarín*, 4 May, "They attacked outside the war zone"). Journalists are not permitted access to the survivors and the narration of this last episode stays in the hands of Argentina's official press agency, TELAM. In a press conference, General Headquarters' press secretary gives details: "When the ship was attacked, it had been carrying out a reconnaissance mission, which made it even more defenceless against the submarine torpedoes it couldn't capture on its radar" (*Clarín*, 6 May, "Emotional arrival of the survivors"; *La Nación*, 6 May, "600 survivors arrive in Ushuaia").

The first lists of survivors' names are distributed only on 7 May (*Clarín*, 7 May, "The first list of survivors distributed"; *La Nación*, 7 May, "We receive the names of survivors"). Testimonials by the protagonists are published between 7 and 9 May (*Clarín*, 7 May, "A shipwrecked sailor speaks"; *La Nación*, 8 May, "The dramatic story of the attack and the hours following"). This continuity in the narration of the events is unexpectedly interrupted as of 9 May with a water-tight military information blackout. Published reports about the cruiser only appear again between 12 and 15 May. These final reports correspond to the end of the account about the sinking, with the definitive names of victims and their sea-burial. General Headquarters closes the narrative circle, by indicating that rescue attempts were finished, in an austere communiqué, no. 49: "The GH informed last night that 770 sailors were rescued alive. Twenty dead and three hundred disappeared is the most tragic count in the war history of the Argentine Navy" (*Clarín*, 15 May, "The victims of the *General Belgrano*: Twenty dead and three hundred missing").

The gravity of the sinking, which was the most controversial action in the war, and the one that caused the greatest single loss of human life in the entire conflict, puts the British press's treatment of it on front stage. In British news territory, then, we can observe both the written and televised press's enunciative strategies. Hastings and Jenkins note that the attack on the *General Belgrano* marked a critical stage in the escalation of the conflict and that this escalation had been approved of by Prime Minister Thatcher. Attacking the ship represented an important victory and allowed the British fleet to dominate the sea around the Malvinas. In the aftermath, however, this action led to finger-pointing at Mrs Thatcher's cabinet, particularly in terms of the speed with which it ordered a step that led Great Britain to sacrifice the greatest number of lives lost at one time in the war (Hastings and Jenkins 1983: 170). "The destruction of the Argentine ship was perhaps the most controversial act in the Falklands fighting" was also pointed out by Glasgow University Media Group (1985: 29).[3]

One of Britain's first reports of the event was given by the private television station, ITN, which contextualised the information within the political frame of the authorisation to sink an Argentine cruiser found outside of the zone of exclusion:

> The attack [...] took place in the late afternoon and was said to be fully in accordance with the rules of engagement of the British forces in the South Atlantic. But it is thought the submarine attack came following a direct order from London, rather than from the Task Force commander Sandy Woodward. (ITN, 3 May, news bulletin, 17:00)

In the days following the sinking, the ensuing worldwide debate about who had given the attack order directly implicated the British Prime Minister, Defence Minister John Nott and Fleet Admiral Lewin. The contradictions that existed in the political game of official British information strategies were placed in evidence. It was demonstrated to what point the British media placed itself in the position, and gave itself the power, to interrogate those directly responsible in the war. This situation was completely different from that of Argentina, where a news blackout reigned.

Let us look at some examples in which the construction of the possible British media world mixes in principal political figures, who become direct information sources:

> Tom Dalyell MP: When the Prime Minister referred to political control, did she herself personally and explicitly authorise the firing of the torpedoes on the IB?
> Prime Minister: I can assure the right honourable gentleman that the Task Force is and was under full political control. (BBC2, 4 May)[4]

---

[3] All British televised news bulletins about the sinking are referenced in Glasgow University Media Group 1985: 316-47.

[4] The same report is found in Adams 1986: 92. The Glasgow University Media Group affirms that the report stating that the order to attack came directly

The opposition was also worried that the Task Force commanders may not be under great enough political control. Mr. Nott revealed today that it was the submarine commander who decided to fire the torpedo which sunk the GB, that he did so – said Mr. Nott – within rules approved by the Cabinet. (ITN, 5 May)

Journalist: "Can you tell us whether the sinking of the GB was done on a political initiative or whether it was purely on the initiative of the commander of the submarine who sank her?"

Sir Lewin: "Of course it was done by Ministerial rules of engagement which were approved by Ministers. We don't go around sinking ships without Ministerial approval." (BBC2, 7 May)

The Glasgow University Media Group (1985: 57) has noted that the British media framed the story of the sinking within a general coverage strategy that touches other aspects of the controversy about Argentine and British source information.

British Journalist in Argentina: "The Military Junta's version of the submarine attack contradicts British reports that the Argentine cruiser posed a significant threat to the fleet. A communiqué tells us that the GB was torpedoed outside the zone declared by both countries around the Falkland Islands. When the Argentine people are being told about hostilities on television or on radio or in the newspapers, it differs vastly from the accounts in Britain, dismissed here as propaganda. The official communiqués continue to claim, after Saturday's attacks (May 1st.), a complete victory for the Argentine forces, with the shooting down of 11 Harrier jets and two helicopters and severe damage cause to the aircraft carrier Hermes and four frigates also hit. Newspapers tell of the triumph of the Argentine forces and other headlines speak of the withdrawal of the enemy. The Argentine press, during war emergencies, is subject to

---

from the British war cabinet appeared in the British press only as of the month of October, once the war was over. The vague and contradictory information from official British sources placed into circulation in the moments following the sinking of the *General Belgrano* was questioned by the same British media, but not by the Argentine one. "The government was reported at the time as stating that the cruiser was sunk on the initiative of the submarine later it was revealed in the US and British press that the order to torpedo the GB had come directly from the war cabinet. According to the *Guardian*, in October, the rules of engagement were 'promptly changed' to permit the attack" (1985: 46).

certain censorship, with journalists facing sanctions for reports undermining national morale. Today, however, details of the submarine attack on the Argentine cruiser were covered, but on inside pages with little prominence." (BBC1, 3 May, 18.00)

Before the number of victims and the amplitude of the naval tragedy were known, the popular British press greeted the sinking with a pronounced level of nationalism, well illustrated in *The Sun*'s infamous headline, "Gotcha". *The Times* of 5 May presented the action as "probably" having been ordered by Task Force command and the *Sunday Times* of 9 May carried the report with a cognitive frame, according to which the cause of the sinking was that the *Conqueror*, in order to avoid revealing its position, had been unable to communicate directly with the War Cabinet. As such, the "crucial blow was delivered without consultation, political or otherwise".

For their part, US newspapers published the story with a lag of twenty-four hours, thereby permitting them to emphasise the number of dead and lost on their front page headlines:

New York Daily News: "Fear 500 Died on Cruiser".
New York Post: "Fear Hundreds Dead in Sea Battle".
Washington Post: "Argentine War Ship Sinks, 900 Missing".

The official British source information strategy was highly evasive and confused in terms of the precise number of victims. It supported this lack of clarity on the official news blackout extant in Argentina:

Journalist: "The GB was safe from immediate destruction by her thick armour plating below the waterline; but for that there might have been loss of life amongst her crew of 1000 men. As yet we don't know exactly when she went down, presumably her two escorting destroyers were able to go alongside to take off the survivors, [...] So, victory once again for the Task Force." (BBC2, 3 May)

Reporter in Argentina: "Officially the government here is saying absolutely nothing about survivors. What we do know [...] the ship normally has a crew of about 1,000 to maybe 1,200 men. Local radio is saying the boat is missing with only 500 men on board. Now it could be that the other five or six hundred were rescued in time, but officially we really don't know." (BBC2, 3 May, *Newsnight Special*)

The Glasgow University Media Group analysed the language used on television for coverage of the sinking. Working on the distinction between "survivors" and "casualties", it found that reporting the number of dead was generally avoided, so as to highlight those that were saved. In the British media agenda of 3 to 15 May, the term "casualties" was used only 11 times on BBC and ITN transmissions, while the term "survivors" was used 77 times. In the construction of the possible British media world, these same media presented the sinking as due to a "threat" 28 times, the British as the aggressors in the sinking 6 times, and the sinking having taken place outside of the zone of exclusion 13 times.

The official Argentine information strategy did not take advantage of the contradictions in the British press, nor did it attempt to focus controversy on the political value that the sinking of the cruiser represented. Post-war analysts demonstrate that, in effect, the British military strategy ended negotiations about the withdrawal of both forces and gave the green light for the military escalation that would culminate with the Argentine surrender on 14 June.

In Adams' analysis,

> This later debate centred on the timing of the sinking in relation to the peace plan put forward by President Belaunde Terry of Peru: it was in effect claimed – and disputed –- that the Prime Minister authorized the attack on the GB in order to scuttle the peace talks. [...] The degree of uncertainty is demonstrable by the fact that *HMS Conqueror* fired not two, but three torpedoes – but one missed. There was no intention to minimize – or maximize – casualties: the *Conqueror*'s aim was to ensure that the GB was put out of action. (1986: 91-2)

This point of view coincides with Cardoso's:

> The Argentine military had taken the conflict far away enough – in both words and deeds – so that it could brusquely step back before the first important slip. For the military, it was unthinkable to suppose that the sinking of the *Belgrano* would operate as a tranquillizer. They thought, as it finally happened, that there would be an exacerbation of a fighting spirit. (Cardoso *et al.* 1983: 231)

Gavshon and Rice conclude that is unimportant if Margaret Thatcher and her war cabinet were poorly informed about Belaunde's proposals (and the direction of the *General Belgrano*). A decision to scare Argentina with the most energetic military means had been taken and the *General Belgrano* was, unfortunately, the first target to fall into this plan's path. Thatcher and her ministers seemed to want a total victory and, after the sinking of the *General Belgrano*, the Argentine Navy effectively ceased to be an active player in the actual fighting (Gavshon and Rice 1984: 206-208).

The Sinking of the *Sheffield*

At 11:04 on the morning of 4 May, two Argentine Navy pilots, members of the Super Etendard Squadron, carried out a low-level surprise flight and simultaneously fired their Exocet missiles at the British destroyer *Sheffield*, sinking it. The meteorological conditions were poor. The planes re-fuelled in flight and returned to their Argentine base without any immediate British reaction.[5]

The *Sheffield*, a high-tech British ship, cost Great Britain 150 million dollars and had a crew of 268, of which 30 died. According to Navy Captain Sam Salt, one of the missiles hit two-and-half metres above the water-line, near the engine room "The port-holes burst, the stairs came undone and a black bitter smoke began to fill the lower decks" (*Clarín*, 5 May, "Argentina sunk a destroyer and brought down two planes"; *La Nación*, 5 May, "London recognises the sinking of the powerful destroyer *Sheffield*"). The episode, which "caused consternation for Prime Minister Margaret Thatcher", was immediately recognised in an official communiqué emitted by the British Ministry of Defence (*Clarín*, 5 May, "The British destroyer *Sheffield* was sunk").

In the account of the destroyer's sinking, one of the paradoxes of official Argentine military source information stands out, as does its lack of a coherent information strategy. No official Argentine communiqué reported the action – doubtless one of the most daring of the entire war – and the confirmation of the event was received from British sources! On 5 and 6 May, the Argentine national press found itself still busy describing the sinking survivor-rescue efforts of the *ARA General Belgrano*. The narration about the GB takes space and relevance away from the attack on and sinking of the *Sheffield*. The narration of the events is placed in the hands of unidentified Argentine naval sources:

---

[5] For a reconstruction of the event, see Gavshon and Rice 1984: 157-9; Hastings and Jenkins 1983: 173-5; Moro 1985: 235-45; Cardoso *et al.* 1983: 244-6.

Argentine naval sources, cited by the DYN agency, gave details about the way in which a British ship was sunk and said that another unit in the Fleet may have suffered serious damage, though they could not yet confirm the latter. The sources stated that while British *Sea Harrier* planes were attacking Port Darwin, and the enemy fleet was concentrating its efforts on this action, a squadron formed of three supersonic Mirage bombers and a Super-Etendard plane of French manufacture resolutely flew toward two ships found between the Malvinas Islands and the continent, with the goal of acting: as a "radar connection" between the bulk of the fleet and its planes. The Super-Etendard, protected by the three Mirage, fired an Exocet missile, which was propelled 35 kilometres until it hit the *Sheffield*. (*Clarín,* 5 May, "The British destroyer *Sheffield* was sunk")

For its part, *La Nación*'s report did not differ substantially from *Clarín*'s. Both, after all, used unidentified Navy sources:

An Exocet missile, of French fabrication, caused the sinking of a British ship, identified by the British Ministry of Defence as the *Sheffield*. The rocket, at a particular distance from its target, began to auto-direct itself, and it was necessary to correct its direction. It was fired by one of the Navy's Super Etendard planes, according to military sources, although these sources explained that this rocket can also be fired from a Mirage. The sinking was not confirmed by General Headquarters, as the plane returned to base after the firing without having been able to observe its ultimate result. (*La Nación,* 5 May, "The counter-offensive launched against the invading fleet")

The only anticipatory report on the air action is General headquarters' communiqué no. 23, published at 00:45 hours on 4 May. It contextualises the military action in a larger narration of the events:

GH communicates that, given the British air attack on Puerto Argentino at 5:30 hours, and in use of its right of legitimate defence, it ordered an air attack on the British Task Force, located 60 miles to the Southeast of the Malvinas. Said attack took place at 10:50 hours with a naval-air force, covered by Air Force planes. The results of this attack are as yet unknown. At 13:00 hours, a British attack took place on Port Darwin, in which two of its Sea Harrier planes were brought down, as here announced in GH's communiqué no. 23. (Complete version in *La Nación,* 5 May,

"Communiqué no. 23"; partial version in *Clarín*, 5 May, "Two British planes brought down")

While the account centred on the sinking of the *ARA General Belgrano* and emotional profiles and personal testimony, the narration of the sinking of the *Sheffield* had the press presenting technical information and the opinions of weapons experts, such as had occurred in circulation of the *Superb* rumour. The French press took up this technical narrative, given that the weapon used was a French one.[6] If the repercussion of the biggest action on the Argentine side was framed in a military information blackout, and the Argentine press had to centre its reports around the technical specificities of the ship, then what was the presentation strategy used by the British press?

The repercussions of British public opinion about the *Sheffield*'s sinking were enormous. Hastings and Jenkins note that exaggerating the impression that the loss of the *Sheffield* produced among the Task Force would have been difficult. Both officers and troops were dumbstruck by the ease with which an enemy plane, using an inexpensive missile and no ultramodern equipment, had destroyed a British warship specifically fitted for anti-air defence. The incident gave evidence to the fact that technology was not all-mighty (1983: 176).

Broadcast programmes were interrupted by a communiqué from the Ministry of Defence, delivered by its press secretary, Ian MacDonald:

> "In the course of its duties within the total exclusion zone around the Falklands Islands, *HMS Sheffield*, a type-42 destroyer, was attacked and hit late this afternoon by an Argentine missile. The ship caught fire which spread out of control. When there was no longer any hope of saving the ship, the ship's company abandoned ship. All those who abandoned were picked up. It is feared there has been a number of casualties, but we have no details of them as yet. Next of kin will be informed first as soon as details are received." (BBC1, 5 April, 9.00)[7]

---

[6] In French newspapers: *Libération*, 5 May, "L'èlectronique mène la guerre. Les militaires du monde entier suivent les combats dans l'Atlantique-Sud, véritable terrain de test pour toute la génération d'armes de l'après-Vietnam"; *Le Monde*, 6 May, "La destruction de l'escorteur britannique *Sheffield*. La première sortie en combat du Super Etendard"; *Point*, 10 May, "Malouines: et soudain la Navy..."; *Figaro Actualité*, 15 May, "Guerre des Malouines: 'on nous a pris pour des indiens avec des arcs et des flèches', disent les argentins".

[7] As in the sinking of the *General Belgrano*, the cited British reports can be found

Stories, Sinkings and Torpedoes

The way the British press covered the destruction of one of its principal warships, and the largest loss of life that it suffered during the conflict, sharply contrasts with the mitigation strategy it used in the account of the *General Belgrano*'s sinking. According to the Glasgow University Media Group, the type of press coverage permits forming the hypothesis that British military authorities directly intervened in how the report about the *Sheffield* was presented, and specifically suggested that it not be labelled a "disaster".

Despite this intervention, it was unavoidable that television put forth not only the political consequences that an event of such magnitude signified for the British Armed Forces, but also the very nature of the tragedy:

> Defence correspondent: "That announcement is going to come as a devastating blow to the Task Force commander and to the Navy, and indeed to Mrs Thatcher. The lost *HMS Sheffield*, one of our newest ships in the fleet, is an astonishing loss to have to admit." (BBC1, 4 May, 21:10)

> Presenter 1: "And in view of tonight's terrible news ..."
> Presenter 2: "Let's leave tonight, just for the moment, the dreadful news of the sinking of the *Sheffield*." (BBC2, 4 May, *Newsnight*)

We can highlight the immediate contextualisation of the story within a political strategy, which was a constant of the British media and which had already occurred in the sinking of the *General Belgrano*. Once again, the legitimacy of the media was founded not only in its information-giving practice, but also in its interpretation of, and questioning about, political leaders' role in the direction of the war. Referring to the direct censorship that Task Force Captains had over reporters travelling with them, David Morrison and Howard Tumber account that, aboard the *Invincible*, two reports by journalist John Witherow were objected to:

> I wrote that a petty officer had told me that, after the *Sheffield* was hit, he no longer thought that the Argies were a bunch of bean-eaters and they were perhaps the best-equipped military forces in South America. The Captain's secretary asked me to change this, on

---

in their complete versions in Glasgow University Media Group 1985: Appendix III. The same version is in Adams 1986: 94.

the Captain's request, to say instead [...] that they were well equipped – to soften it mainly because he knew the crew was reading it. [...] There was much greater censorship, we were told less and less, and the frustration just grew constantly and we complained much harder. On occasions the Captain was dragged out of his bunk at night and stopped stories. (Morrison and Tumber 1988: 39-43)

Given the censorship of "D news", however, the story of the sinking basically slid to informing about casualties, as had occurred in the case of the *General Belgrano*. In an analysis carried out by Valerie Adams, British television was found to have focused its attention on the way that the *Sheffield* was sunk and on loss of human life (Adams 1986: 94).

> Reporter: "The number of sailors who perished still stands at about thirty. [...] Next of kin are being informed and we expect a list of those who perished later this afternoon." (BBC1, 5 May, 12:30)

From the beginning of the coverage, the theme of death and human tragedy filled the press, in opposition to its self-censorship in the construction of the possible media world of the *General Belgrano*. During the period running from 4 to 9 of May, British television used the term "perished" 62 times and the term "survivors" only 31 times (Glasgow University Media Group 1985: 42).

Descriptive content, present in the Argentine press's account of the event, could equally be found in the commentaries of the televised British media.

> "Built by Vickers and Barrow, *HMS Sheffield* was commissioned in 1975. She carried one Lynx helicopter fitted with Sea Skewer missiles and the ship herself was armed with Sea Dart missiles. The Sea Dart were very sophisticated and in order to combat Argentine Exocet missiles the *Sheffield* would have needed the short-wave Sea Wolf system." (ITN, 4 May, 22:10)

> "*HMS Sheffield* was the first of the Royal Navy's type-42 destroyers and didn't have the anti-missile weapon that was fitted to later types of warships. This might have saved her from attack by a modern, French-built, Super Etendard fighter bomber equipped with the Exocet missile, only fairly recently delivered to the Argentine by the French." (BBC1, 5 May, 12:30)

Stories, Sinkings and Torpedoes

The Argentine military source information strategy, and its favoured use by the newspapers, for the coverage of information concerning the attack on the *General Belgrano,* did not sufficiently take advantage of the event's political consequences, especially in light of its gravity within the international community. For its part, though, the sinking of the *Sheffield* stayed only one day on the papers' agendas and did not accentuate – aside from concordant descriptions about military technology – the consequences of the Argentine action on British public opinion.

In the shared opinions of Adams and the Glasgow University Media Group about the coverage of these two events in the British press, the explanatory frame adopted by Great Britain was one in which she was not directly responsible for either action. In a tactic of putting responsibility elsewhere – be it in the attack of the *General Belgrano,* or the lack of defence on the *Sheffield* – official British source information was centred on the idea that it had suffered a direct act of aggression:

> The loss of the *Sheffield* was in several ways a turning point in the commentary on the Falklands conflict, particularly following so closely on the sinking of *General Belgrano*. The media now saw that the fighting was for real: "bloodless brutality was not practical". (Adams 1986: 95)

The two governments and their respective media systems found themselves symmetrically positioned. As had happened in the sinking of the *General Belgrano,* with the British war cabinet and the Argentine soul, the sinking of the *Sheffield* stopped the peace negotiations spearheaded by Peru and blocked the mediation of United Nations Secretary, Javier Pérez de Cuéllar. As Cardoso points out,

> Several persons tied to the conflict with Great Britain expressed to the authors, once the war was over, that Argentina's success in sinking the *Sheffield* was likely the final obstacle to arriving at a negotiated solution. The Argentine military's spirit here showed itself as a triumphalistic state that did not match a dispassionate analysis of what the future might bring. (1983: 245)

In effect, while the Argentine Minister of Foreign Affairs, Nicanor Costa Méndez, was giving a press conference at the United Nations and affirming, "We are willing to negotiate, negotiate and negotiate in order to find a peaceful solution", British Chancellor Francis Pym was declaring before the House of Commons: "The government will veto any UN resolution or a ceasefire in the Southern Atlantic", and

Argentine Defence Minister Amadeo Frugoli was stating: "The Argentine government is ready to do battle wherever and whenever" (*La Prensa*, 5 May, "Pym ends his mission in the UN" ; 6 May, "The Chancery's response").

On 8 May, Great Britain extended its blockade by a distance of 12 maritime miles. Defence Minister John Nott threatened to bomb Argentina's continental air bases. The decision to send a British landing force to the Malvinas-Falklands had been taken. Operation Sutton was beginning.

Epilogue

The Double Reader

On the dawn of 21 May, at the beginning of the pincer movement to surround Puerto Argentino [Port Stanley], the British forces disembarked in San Carlos (Soledad Island) to set up a bridgehead. The advance of the Navy's professional troops and of the British Army's mercenaries towards the capital city would last twenty-three days. They found themselves delayed by the awful terrain, which prevented quick movements, by the harshness of the weather, logistical problems and, above all, by the attacks of the Argentine Air Force, which sank and damaged a number of war ships and frigates.[1] The Argentine defence, essentially made up of Navy and Army infantry troops, the majority of whom were soldiers still in training, fought and resisted in Puerto Darwin and Prado de Ganso [Goose Green] (28 and 29 May), Mount Kent (1 June), Mount Longdon, Cerros Dos Hermanas and Harriet (11 and 12 of June), the plateau of Wireless Ridge and the highlands of Tumbledown and Williams (13 and 14 June) at the entrance of Puerto Argentino [Port Stanley].[2]

It was not the aim of my research to assess either the defence's military actions or the strategies followed by the Argentine Armed Forces, which were judged by their peers in due course.[3] I would like only to point out here two elements which I think summarise well the development of the news during the last two weeks of the conflict: the construction of the figure of "the wait" and the reiteration of the "calculated risk" hypothesis in the formation of the media possible world of the military communiqués and of the press in general.

---

[1] For a reconstruction of the last two weeks of the military operations in the Falklands-Malvinas, see Moro 1985: 287-343; Hastings and Jenkins 1983: 221ff.; Joffre and Aguiar 1987: 137ff.; and Ruiz Moreno 1986: 133-7.
[2] For the logistical difficulties encountered by the British operation and the Argentine defence, see Thompson 1985; Hastings and Jenkins 1983: 307ff.; Joffre and Aguiar 1987: 130, 138-45.
[3] *Comisión Investigadora de las Responsabilidades Políticas y Estratégicas Militares del Conflicto en el Atlántico Sur* (CAERCAS) [Commission in charge of the Investigation of the Military Strategic and Political Responsibilities in the South Atlantic]; Joffre and Aguiar 1987: 57-60; Hastings and Jenkins 1983: 307, 334-7. For an evaluation of the two countries' war strategies, see Ruiz Moreno 1986: 164-6. On the static nature of the Argentine defence, see Gavshon and Rice 1984: 64-9. On the exhaustion of the Argentine resistance, see Cardoso *et al.* 1983: 275, 294, 363-6; and Joffre and Aguiar 1987: 275.

In my previous analyses I have emphasised the strategies of construction of the media truth through the circulation of alternative possible worlds, the efforts of the Argentine press to distance itself from the information from textual military sources in a censorship situation and the design of Model Readers, the comparison of the information treatment by Argentine and British media, and the information controversy between Argentine and British official textual sources in the construction of an essentially polemic discourse. In short, I have attempted to demonstrate that what we call "information" in a conflict situation is a complex nebula of inaccuracies, approximations, inferences and negotiations which reach the reader on a daily basis, supporting their illusion of consumption of current affairs. This type of information seems to be the tip of the iceberg of a certain "unsaid" and "untold", and the reader goes along groping in the dark of the media interpretative system, consuming stories and deciphering a plurality of voices which coexist under the wide coverage of the news.

Studying the different versions of the final days in the islands, reading the testimonies of the war's participants, placing myself deliberately in the site of who is reconstructing a story – the news stories of those days – I feel obliged to give a warning: the media, with their own sources along with the military sources, constructed an account approximate to the facts for the simple reason that the communications amongst the troops which resisted the British advance were cut off.[4] This does not absolve those responsible in the media –

[4] Conscript José María Lambertini – combatant of the Air Defence Artillery's group GADA 601 during the Falklands-Malvinas war – contributes the following story: "We had a military team radio which communicated our position. Through this radio we also used to listen to Buenos Aires and Uruguayan radio stations, but the transmissions were bad. In the evenings, while in the trench, we used to listen to the World Cup that was taking place in Spain. We could listen to news that said that we were winning, and we thought that the British were destroying us, only retarded people could believe something like that. But we got practically no information; at war you cannot use the radio, so as not to reveal your position. This happened during the last few days, before the surrender, they were already there. When they ordered us to fall back, we abandoned our positions, leaving everything behind – guns, helmets, everything we had – and we ran towards the town. On our way there we found an Air Force shed full of food! And also the Kelpers' houses – which had been abandoned – and there we hid, in desperation. I remember that in one of those houses there was a tape recorder and we sat down there to listen to The Rolling Stones. At midnight, the British arrived and they made us their prisoners" (interview in Rosario, 12 January 1991).

nor does it absolve the military spokesmen – but it does contribute to put into perspective our understanding of the production of news disseminated during the last days within a general framework of information blackout, a situation which was in fact shared by Argentines and British.[5]

It is this lack of information what allows us better to understand the characteristics of the information provided by the Argentine press during the days prior to the defeat: total homogeneity of the stories in the news media, with only one textual source and the increasing impoverishment of information, no use of their own sources, dominance of the military communiqués. On the other hand, I do not think that the Argentine press analysed here – the newspapers *Clarín* and *La Nación* – can be said to have acted with a triumphalistic and irresponsible attitude which would prevent the reader from inferring the ending. On the contrary, I would like to highlight precisely the complex communication strategies employed by these media to put into effect a set of narrative programmes centred on the construction of alternative possible worlds, in order to sustain the media contract established with their readers.

During the last two weeks of the conflict, the two trends that have been outlined in the course of other information episodes became more pronounced. *La Nación* and *Clarín* – beyond the differences in their respective constructions of enunciative and narrative strategies – repeated the chosen formula: military textual source + own textual source + British textual source, thus constructing a reader who waits for the development of the events. It is not necessary to reiterate here the extent to which the British information was controlled and inaccurate. The information from Argentine military sources also repeated previous formulae, spreading appeasing slogans in its attempt to construct a reader who waits too, but trustingly waits for the victory. Let us have a quick look at some examples:

---

[5] See Hastings and Jenkins 1983: 353-5. On the British losses caused by the Argentine Air Force, which were kept secret in order not to demoralise the British home front, see Hastings and Jenkins 1983: 305; and Joffre and Aguiar 1987: 121. General Joffre, in his testimony, tells us that whilst the British media did not broadcast news either of the attack areas or the losses suffered, the Argentine media emphatically made public that all the British attacks to/on the airport had been resisted, this being the reason why the British carried on bombing it. On the lack of a psychological war strategy in the Argentine media, from the Army's viewpoint, see Joffre and Aguiar 1987: 167.

(a) *the model of the reader who waits*

"The analysts estimate that the decisive battle for the control of Puerto Argentino [Port Stanley] could take place in the next few hours" (*Clarín*, 31 May, "The invading forces consolidate their position in Darwin and Ganso Verde [Goose Green]").

"While waiting for the ground battle to take place and while military analysts consider that this will be the decisive battle, the Argentine troops remained tense and on guard in Puerto Argentino [Port Stanley]" (*La Nación*, 1 June, "British outposts are 25km from Puerto Argentino [Port Stanley]").

"On the surrender of Ganso Verde [Goose Green] and Puerto Darwin [Port Darwin] – according to what *Clarín* could get to learn from a responsible source [...] " (*Clarín*, 1 June, "They fight near Puerto Argentino [Port Stanley]").

(b) *the model of the reader who trustingly waits*

"According to military sources the majority of the British have been brought down on the beach" (*La Nación*, 22 May, "Major losses of the enemy in yesterday's combats").

"We are in a clearly favourable position" (*Clarín*, 22 May, "Frugoli: we are in a favourable position").

"Military sources affirmed that the British are retreating and that the action has leant in favour of the Argentine forces" (*La Nación,* 29 May, "40% of their troops are out of combat").

"The Argentine leadership has carried out studies on the possible advances of the enemy. That's to say, the surrender of Puerto Darwin [Port Darwin] and Ganso Verde [Goose Green] is within their plans, since the political-military aim of outmost importance is Puerto Argentino [Port Stanley]" (*Clarín,* 1 June, "They are fighting near Puerto Argentino [Port Stanley]").

What is interesting about these examples is that contradictory versions simultaneously coexist in both newspapers; as macro-enunciators, they leave room for the circulation of alternative and opposing voices. But actually what this plural strategy produces, for the recipient, is the simultaneous construction of a double reader, in the same way that the possible media worlds that circulated in the *Superb* or *Lagartos [Lizards]* episodes were double. It is the presence of this double reader what allows for the fictionalisation effect to finish and close. In this respect, the discourse from military textual source appears as an insertion within the news discourse of the media, thus performing a linking or staggering function without the newspaper ever allowing it to merge.

The Double Reader

The newspapers – as macro-enunciators of a plurality of voices – by never yielding their framing power in the production of the news, constructed at most two alternative worlds and, correspondingly, two opposing sets of readers. It would seem that one of the explanations of how news discourse works in situations of conflict and generalised censorship might be precisely this operation of simultaneous construction of a double reader: that of Power and that of the Media. The news Media Contract reminds us once again that the primary loyalty of the reader is always directed towards the journalistic enunciation and that the newspaper has the power of fixing and halting the virtually unlimited web of possible interpretations, simply by means of an adequate use of the inverted commas and of the textual sources.

On the one hand, it produces a reader obedient to the imposed narrative programme, a "reader-prisoner" of the "Malvinisation" of information syndrome. On the other hand, it constructs another type of reader who, on the contrary, has the ability to compare and contrast different versions, a reader who has actually been constructed out of the image of the journalist, because in the same way the latter is forced to check different sources and versions in order to organise their own cognitive process. The news Media Contract also produces its own Model Reader by mirroring its own information performance.

It would seem that in media societies, essentially based on the principle of circulation, absolute censorship does not exist. In the Argentine case, even though there was strict information control, the press operated during the whole conflict with the relative freedom of constructing opposing readers. One could conclude that censorship cases can be identified whenever a media story becomes, by definition, monolithic, that is to say, when it presents only one textual source of information which is accepted by all the media as their own, producing only one possible reader. However, this did not happen in the newspapers analysed here during the Malvinas-Falklands war. Insofar as the existence and circulation in the media of at least two readers are possible, censorship, by definition, cannot any longer be said to exist, even if the control of the news contents still exists.

Clarín and *La Nación*, even if accepting the space granted to military sourced discourses, introduced other textual sources and constructed their own strategies of enunciative legitimisation. By not allowing the military discourse to merge with that of the media and thus omitting to constitute an only subject of enunciation – the dream of any totalitarian discourse – by setting the enunciative boundaries between their own textual sources, the official and the quasi-official ones, by having recourse to and making use of the narrative device of embedding "I narrate (and they tell)", *Clarín* and *La Nación* were able to detach themselves from the war and to open up some space for other political voices which emerged immediately after the defeat.[6]

The British veto

On 5 June the United Kingdom, along with the vote of the United States, vetoed the ceasefire motion proposed by Spain and Panama at the Security Council meeting. Despite the fact that Argentina had obtained the minimum necessary consent in favour, of nine countries and the abstention of four, the United Kingdom made use of its power to veto, followed by the United States, which belatedly wanted to change its vote for an abstention. Too late. The Argentine representative to the United Nations, Ambassador Enrique Ros, made the United Kingdom directly responsible for the continuation of the conflict. The diplomatic observers estimated that Britain's attitude was to achieve an absolute military victory (*La Nación,* 6 May, "Great Britain and the USA vetoe the ceasefire motion in the U. N.").[7]

This episode became the turning point that made possible the change of information strategy in the days that immediately preceded the Argentine surrender. *Clarín* and *La Nación* began to sketch for the first time a little world linked to the forms of the Argentine withdrawal, whilst the Model Reader of the military discourse started to notice that their fate and that of the Military Junta's were inextricably tied to a success in the final battle for the Malvinas-Falklands.

> The Argentine garrison was reinforced and it is in good condition for the defence. Nevertheless, it is estimated that the aggressors' offensive may begin in the short term. In military circles it was

---

[6] On the very same day, 15 June, *Clarín* published the document made public by Raul Alfonsín in disagreement with the leadership of his party, the Radical Civic Union. He states: "The Armed Forces do not deserve this fate and Argentina does not deserve this government [...]. The government must resign and, right now, a period of civilian transition to democracy must begin" (*Clarín,* 15 June, "Two points of view within the Radical Civic Union"). The Justicialist Party, on the other hand, attempts to put forward a proposal for the post-war period within a debate about the restructuring of the party. Amongst the names of those in charge of this renewal, Carlos Menem and Antonio Cafiero appear (*La Nación,* 14 June, "The Peronist Party is preparing for the post-war period").
[7] In an interview for this book, Ambassador Atilio Molteni states: "Whilst the British had it clear that they had to get rid of us, we assumed that the United States would have prevented an Argentine defeat, but this was not the case."

stated that "to resist until the last man in Puerto Argentino [Port Stanley] goes beyond the strictly military sphere to become something political". (*La Nación*, 6 May, "Intense Argentine Air Bombing")

" [...] that allows an honourable and dignified exit from the crisis". *(La Nación,* 6 May, "Admiral Moya said that the conflict will be long")

"[...] Britain is preparing its post-war process and the reconciliation with Argentina". (*Clarín*, 6 May, "Britain and Its Allies", article signed by Francois Lepot)

Five days before the Argentine surrender, in a desperate discursive action to save his own government and his readers, General Galtieri declared in an exclusive interview with the Spanish newspaper *Ya:*

"Argentina and its people, and I'm sure supported by Spanish America and many other peoples of the world, are willing to carry on with the war for the months and years that may become necessary." (*La Nación*, 9 June, "The war shall continue for as long as necessary")

In the dialogue between official sources, Margaret Thatcher responded with another threat: "The British troops will have to take by force the Argentine bastions in the Malvinas/Falkland Islands" (*La Nación,* 9 June, "Total intransigence from Margaret Thatcher"). And the Model Reader of the military possible world knew that they could still wait trustingly because "all the elements enter their 'maximum tension and play in the next few days, but not in the next few hours, as had been anticipated at the beginning of this week', confirms an unidentified military source" (*La Nación*, 9 June, "A war which combines past and present").[8]

"With eyes filled with tears"
Then, the Pope arrived. John Paul II travels to Argentina and stays there for forty-eight hours. This visit, whose coverage is monopolised by the media system, allows *Clarín* and *La Nación* to move away from

---

[8] On the Argentine government's belief in the improbability of a British final attack and in the continuation of the war, see Cardoso *et al.* 1983: 284, 301.

the topic of the war and to change the agenda. As a matter of fact, on 11, 12 and 13 June – twenty-four hours after the Argentine surrender – the topic of the war appears relegated to the final pages of the main sections of both newspapers, and other voices appear in the public arena and in the newspapers' headlines. The small world function of the mini-story of the Pope's visit reveals itself as immensely useful because – beyond the historical and political importance that this first visit had within the tradition of the papal mediations in Argentine border conflicts – it enabled the transformation of the Model Reader who waits for the resolution of the war to a Model Reader who was prepared for the defeat.

The Argentine Church organised the papal visit under the slogan "For the triumph of peace over war". More than two million people gathered to pray in Palermo Park, in downtown Buenos Aires, accompanying the Pope in his co-celebrated mass. All of a sudden, the radio stations and television channels interrupted the celebration, which was being network broadcast for the whole country, with a communiqué from the Estado Mayor Conjunto [the Military Junta] which announced that the British Army, with 4,500 men, had penetrated the Argentine defences by 3km.[9] The crowds literally roared for several seconds, "We want peace, peace, peace!" The Pope, after finishing the mass, left straight for the airport, asking for a "just, honourable, long-lasting" peace. On the plane steps, after saying goodbye to General Galtieri, he raised his hand and said, by way of farewell, "God bless Argentina", before disappearing in the middle of the photographers' flashes (*La Nación*, 13 June, "An extraordinary demonstration of faith accompanied John Paul II"; *Clarín*, 13 June, "Two million Argentines prayed with the Pope").

During the three days that preceded the surrender, three Model Readers coexist in the newspapers' agenda: the survival of the military possible world's Model Reader who trustingly awaits the ending, the survival of the media possible world's Model Reader who organises its information sources, and a new Reader – enabled to occupy other

---

[9] The military communiqués from the Estado Mayor Conjunto [Military Junta] appeared in *Clarín* in its issue of 15 June. The one that I refer to states: "Communiqué no. 158: The EMC informs that as at 10:30pm of yesterday evening, the British forces restarted their attack in three different points of the battle front, with great display of resources. The fight extended towards the control of Mount Tumbledown and Wireless Ridge, and involved the intervention of the Infantry and Artillery from both sides. Up until now the Argentine forces are containing the attack and are holding their positions."

positions within Argentine society and within the media – because new enunciators who break up the hegemony of the war narrative emerge. The textual topic of the post-war is now ready to start.

"When the papal visit has finished, the citizens will meet again to face the dramatic contingency of the war and the uncertainties of the political future", editorialises *La Nación* on the 13 June, recollecting, in turn, the old issues that lacerated Argentine society before the conflict (*La Nación*, 13 June, "The pilgrim of the difficult times"). The political fate of the Military Junta appears forever anchored to the resolution of the war, and "the end of the war should be followed by an immediate institutional normalisation" (*La Nación*, 13 June, "The Pope, bastings and stitches").

Clarín agreed with *La Nación*'s position. An editorial signed by journalist Joaquín Morales Sola stated: "Nothing ever gathered in Argentina more than two million people in a single event, which demonstrates that there is no social or political organisation in the country that has the capacity of the Catholic Church, and on the other hand, the Pope is for Argentineans the highest moral authority in the planet [...]. He [the Pope] did it in a country which has undergone almost a decade of only listening to the language of war: from the subversive[10] explosion of the early 1970s to the Malvinas-Falklands war now, all through the struggle against insurgency and the war preparations against Chile, the Pope brings a message of peace, human rights and political and social dignity" (*Clarín*, 13 June, "Between prayer and war")

The issue of human rights and of the "disappeared" returns to the newspapers in the assessment that John Paul II himself makes of his visit to Argentina. In a dispatch from the news agency AP, from Rome, and when the journalists asked him whether during his visit he had discussed the issue of the Argentine "disappeared", who had gone missing in the ten previous years because of military repression, the Pope answered: "We have always tried in the past, and will continue in the present, to obtain information about the disappeared" (*Clarín*, 14 June, "The issue of the disappeared"). Argentine public opinion re-encounters, once again, its old and painful, still unsolved narratives.

---

[10] "Subversive" and "subversion" are euphemisms devised during the last Argentine dictatorship to designate the activities of the "extreme left".

The Readers' Revenge

From the military point of view, the reconstruction of the Malvinas-Falklands war has been comprehensively documented by both sides. They fought inch by inch in a trench war up until the Argentines exhausted their men and their munitions, and whole companies were defeated defending the heights on the outskirts of Puerto Argentino.[11] On his return from Ezeiza airport, where he went to say goodbye to the Pope, the last telephone conversation with General Menéndez – up until that point, governor of the islands – was awaiting General Galtieri:

> General – Menéndez said – we have reached the limit of our possibilities: the British are surrounding the town and our heavy artillery is unusable; also, our soldiers can't carry on any longer. They are exhausted.
>
> The British are exhausted too, Menéndez – Galtieri replied – we have to resist, our troops need to be encouraged, they should not be taken out of the trenches in order to go backwards, but they should be taken out of the trenches in order to go forward. We have to counter-attack with courage and enthusiasm.
>
> I think you don't understand, General – the Governor replied. I told you that we were going to give them combat and so we did during the entire night. But this cannot go on any longer.
>
> Regroup the troops and succeed. We have to fight, Menéndez – the President concluded.
>
> General, the Marine Infantry Battalion number 5 – Admiral Otero has just told me – has arrived here with just one commando and one section. Artillery Group number 4 is missing. We have lost all our positions on the mountain
>
> The only thing I can say is that you fight – Galtieri said.[12]

In a famous interview which took place at the same time with Italian independent journalist Oriana Fallaci, Galtieri emphatically asserted: "Whatever happens militarily, whichever the regime that rules the country in the future, be sure that Argentineans will continue

---

[11] On the last combats, see Hastings and Jenkins 1983: 284-335; Cardoso *et al.* 1983: 279ff.; Joffre and Aguiar 1987: 278-81; Ruiz Moreno 1986: 211-35; Moro 1985: 409-88.

[12] For the reconstruction of this dialogue, see Ruiz Moreno 1986: 396; Cardoso *et al.* 1983: 296; Hastings and Jenkins 1983: 346; Joffre and Aguiar 1987: 275.

fighting for the Malvinas. They will not surrender" (*Clarín*, 13 June, "Argentina will continue the struggle"). *Clarín*'s correspondent in London, François Lepot, has commented on the effect of this interview with Galtieri published in *The Times*, which unwittingly established the last dialogue which would take place between institutional textual sources. Margaret Thatcher responded, now magnanimously: "I don't ask for an unconditional surrender of the Argentines, they can withdraw with dignity and in orderly fashion, if they so wish" (*Clarín*, 13 June, "Has the battle begun?").

On 14 June at 7pm, local time, General Menéndez agreed with the commander of the British troops, General Jeremy Moore, on the conditions of the matter-of-fact ceasefire: the recognition of the courage of the Argentine troops, the creation of an Argentine-British joint commission for the acts of transference of the islands' administration, the use of combined forces for the disposal of the minefields, the withdrawal of the Argentine soldiers in charge of their own companies, the non-submission of the Argentine flags to the British Army. On the document, written in English, Menéndez crossed out the word "unconditional" from the statement of surrender, which was not published in any Argentine media.[13]

On the very same 14 June, whilst the BBC in London informs that a ceasefire agreement between the Commanders-in-Chief of both armies had been signed, with the subsequent Argentine rendition, the survival of the military possible world reappears again:

> The military authorities, meanwhile, pointed out that, despite the advances of the British, the situation did not constitute in itself a fact of either success or defeat. (*Clarín*, 14 June, "Bombings on the British outposts")

---

[13] On the conditions of the surrender and the Argentine soldiers' resistance despite the abandonment of their superiors, see Hastings and Jenkins 1983: 308-9, 328, 331. For Argentine versions of the same issues, see Cardoso *et al*. 1983: 298ff.; Joffre and Aguiar 1987: 296-301; and Moro 1985: 493-507. The last communiqué from the Estado Mayor Conjunto [Military Junta] is communiqué no. 164: "The EMC informs that the meeting scheduled for today, 14 June 1982, at 4pm, between the commander of the British ground forces, General Jeremy Moore, and the military governor of the Falkland-Malvinas Islands, General Mario Benjamín Menéndez, has been postponed until 7pm. In this meeting the conditions for the ceasefire must be agreed."

The Interior Minister [Home Office Secretary], General Saint Jean, in his last statement to the press, said:

> "Argentina will not leave the Falklands-Malvinas even if she has to fight all of her life in order to keep them in her patrimony". (*Clarín*, 14 June, "If they take the Falklands-Malvinas again, the hostilities will continue")

Even on 15 June, according to the statements of the Head of the Argentine Air Force – who played the crucial role of defence and attack throughout the war – the surrender had not been acknowledged and the script of the military possible world continued to be intact. Brigadier Basilio Lami Dozo, minimising the consequences, affirms in a press interview:

> "This country will carry on trying to consolidate its re-encountered identity. I believe that all sectors of society, independently from how this episode and the battle of Puerto Argentino [Port Stanley] – *which is just another battle* – get solved, will try to build and consolidate a really important Argentina, with a leading role in the world of the future."
> *Can the war actions continue?*
> "They may continue."
> *Even if losing Puerto Argentino [Port Stanley]?*
> "Don't forget that we have troops in other places on the Falklands-Malvinas." (*Clarín*, 15 June, "The political aim must be consolidated")

Only forty-eight hours after the signing of the Rendition Statement, *La Nación* and *Clarín* publish the conditions of the Argentine retreat, although in the form of a "leak" and a "version":

> Despite the secrecy which surrounded the topic, it became known in military circles about the agreement through which the ceasefire and the withdrawal of troops were established, signed on Monday in Puerto Argentino [Port Stanley] between the governor of the Falkland/Malvinas Islands, General Mario Benjamín Menéndez, and the head of the colonialist forces, General Jeremy Moore. (*La Nación*, 16 June, "The conditions for the ceasefire")

> The statement signed the night before last by the military governor of the Falkland/Malvinas Islands, General Mario Benjamín

Menéndez, and the commander of the British troops consists of seven points, according to versions collected last night in Buenos Aires. (*Clarín*, 16 June, "A British General assumed control of the islands")

The chancellor [Minister of Foreign Affairs] Costa Méndez proposed the resignation of the whole cabinet and presented his resignation verbally, along with Economy Minister Roberto Alemann – the only civilian minister of the government – who thus accompanied the diplomat's gesture. A series of chain meetings was precipitated in the military hierarchies, which criticised the leadership of the war. General Galtieri was then the one in charge of putting the final stop to the story of the military possible world. In a message addressed to the whole country, he stated:

"The battle for Puerto Argentino [Port Stanley] has finished. Our soldiers fought with supreme effort for the dignity of our Nation. Those who fell are forever alive in the heart and in the great history of the Argentines".

Clarín entitles its edition of the 16 June with the headline, "There will be no definitive peace if there is a return to the colonial status, Galtieri said", choosing once again direct speech, whilst *La Nación* publishes on the same day the headline, "Our country's forces retreat from the Falklands-Malvinas", thus positioning itself in the place of the story.

And what about the readers? Galtieri promises, in the first self-criticism of the whole conflict, to revise and correct the mistakes in both home and foreign policies, and so, "we will rescue the Republic, we will reconstruct its institutions, we will re-establish democracy on solid bases of equality and respect". But it is too late. Nobody wants to occupy the space of this plural "we" that claims to be all-inclusive. The script of his fall and that of the whole regime was precipitating rapidly.[14]

In the Plaza de Mayo [May Square] in Buenos Aires, the people cried and shouted, "The military dictatorship will end, will end!" The journalists, who were crowding behind the police, were also blamed. "Tell the truth, tell the truth!" the crowd roared as they threw coins at

---

[14] On General Galtieri's fall, and his inability to understand that the war and his position within the Army and the Military Junta were lost, see Cardoso *et al.* 1983: 301ff.; and Joffre and Aguiar 1987: 315.

the official television vans that were filming the scenes. "You deceived us too!" The police threw tear-gas canisters and 150 people were arrested (*Clarín,* 16 June, "Violence in the Square"; *La Nación,* 16 June, "Serious incidents took place yesterday in several downtown areas").

The story of the Falklands-Malvinas war opens and closes on the same stage, seventy-four days later and with an extra thousand Argentine casualties. The construction of the military possible world, taken up towards the narrative climax of victory, did not foresee an alternative ending. And it is for this reason that the signed surrender could never be published. The Model Readers of this world, presumably present in the Plaza de Mayo, could not bear the anti-climax of disappointment. And in its impossibility to face the fiduciary irreversibility, the regime fell in twenty-four hours, demolished by its own readers.

Conclusion: Constructing Memory

Falklands-Malvinas as Years Go By: From Epics to Anecdote

On the occasion of the twenty-fifth anniversary of the 1982 war between Argentina and Great Britain – under British rule since 1833 and diplomatically claimed by Argentina as forming part of its territory – many books and articles on both sides of the Atlantic have been published. Most of these articles focus on the different interpretations and evaluations of a conflict which confronted for the first time in contemporary history a South American country and NATO's second power, both belonging to the same geo-strategic camp.

What was the evolution of the perceptions about the pertinence of the conflict? And what were the transformations of the public sphere in close relationship to the structural crisis which Argentina went through after the declaration of surrender? My hypothesis states that the re-birth of Argentine democracy in 1983 is undoubtedly a direct result of the Argentine military defeat in June 1982. Twenty-five years later, a deep legitimacy crisis of the Argentine political parties also came about, along with the default crisis (2001) and the crisis of the economic system and the neo-liberal model established during the 1990s.

Twenty-five years on, it is possible to attempt not only an evaluation of a lost war, but also an appraisal of a democratic transition which came to an end on 19 December 2001 with the gigantic *cacerolazo* [pan-banging] that toppled Fernando de la Rua's Radical Civic Union Party government, in an episode of civic protest which has no precedents in our recent history. The slogans "The Falklands-Malvinas are Argentinean, and so too are the disappeared" (1982) and "All out" (2002), open and close this historical period, and sum up the deep transformation in the citizens' public sphere. In the same way that the different components and consequences of the military discourse have been thoroughly analysed, what has yet to be done is a reading of the neoliberal discourse's power as the hegemonic discourse that channelled, through the construction of public opinion of those years, the general perception of the inevitability of an economic model which had devastating consequences for Argentina in particular and for Latin America in general.

Historical Memory

When in March 1982 General Leopoldo Fortunato Galtieri – the third to occupy the Military Junta's presidency – decided to invade the Falklands-Malvinas with the "Rosario Operation", he was seeking to distract the public attention from the delicate economic situation of the country, which by then had an inflation rate of 600%. The plan of disembarking on the islands – "a brutal foreign policy action"[1] – was an extreme attempt to restore credibility and prestige to the dictatorship, but essentially an action internal to the military regime, which was undermined by internal conflicts. Despite the fact that precipitation and surprise were the determining factors of the Argentine strategy,[2] the Army disembarked in Port Stanley, but the British Task Force retook the islands after a 74-day war. The conflict cost Argentina the loss of approximately 904 combatants, 650 Argentines, half of them killed in the sinking of the battleship *General Belgrano*, and 253 British.[3] The defeat in the war against Britain accelerated the end of the military regime, which was led during its final year by General Reynaldo Bignone. The result was the victory of the Radical Civic Union Party candidate Raúl Alfonsín, who made the Military Junta's trials the main agenda of his campaign for the recovery of Human Rights. He thus created the CONADEP (National Commission on the Disappearance of Persons), and inaugurated the rule of law and a democratic transition in a country marked by 17 years of successive military regimes.

Since 1964 the issue of the sovereignty of the Falklands-Malvinas Islands has been discussed in the United Nation's Decolonisation Committee. Argentina based its position on the papal document of 1494 – the Treaty of Tordecillas – by which the colonies of the New World were divided between Spain and Portugal. Subsequently, the islands had been in Argentina's possession since 1826. The British, for their part, substantiated the reasons for their sovereignty on the grounds of their effective possession of the territory, guaranteed by British administration since 1833, and on the assurance of the islanders' right to self-determination, in accordance with what was indicated by the Decolonisation Commission. The British position maintained that, since the end of the colonial period, the Argentines wanted to take

---

[1] *La Nación*, 2 April 2002, "Una crónica íntima del desembarco en Malvinas" ["An intimate chronicle of the landing in the Malvinas"], by Juan Carlos Escribano.
[2] Washington had not been warned of the landing, and the US government's surprise was reflected in *Clarín*'s headline of 3 April: "Reagan: 'I Never Thought They Would Do It'". The Argentine Defence Minister, Amadeo Frugoli, was informed on the eve of the landing; Chancellor Costa Méndez (the Foreign Affairs Minister), on 26 March, when the decision was made.
[3] According to Argentine figures, there were 649 Argentine and 255 British casualties. French sources state that 750 Argentines died in combat (*Le Monde*, 15 March 2002), and Italian sources report 650 fatalities (*L'Unita*, 3 April 2002).

Conclusion: Constructing Memory

control of the islands against their inhabitants' open opposition.

In 1965 the United Nation's General Assembly passed a resolution that invited Great Britain and Argentina to find a peaceful solution to the territorial disagreement. The discussions took place until February 1982. On 19 March of that year, a group of Argentine whalers were caught by the British in the south of the Georgias Islands lifting their national flag. Great Britain immediately prompted the Argentine authorities to remove the fishing ships. The diplomatic escalation increased up until 2 April, when Argentine troops disembarked in the islands in an action planned by Admiral Jorge Anaya. The British representatives retreated to Montevideo. General Mario Benjamín Menéndez was declared governor of the islands, whilst both in Buenos Aires and in the rest of the country the demonstrations against the regime became expressions of solidarity, in support of the "reconquest" war undertaken. The armed action did indeed recover temporarily the people's consensus, but further isolated Argentina on the international front, given that the country had already been strongly questioned for its recurring human rights violations.

On 8 April, American Secretary of State Alexander Haig arrived in London in a mediation attempt which proved unsuccessful, on account of the intransigence of the Argentine military high ranks, which were imbued with triumphalism. At the same time, the European Community passed a number of economic sanctions against Argentina. The United Nations, for its part, declared Argentina as an "invading country", urging it immediately to vacate the islands through its Resolution 502. Whilst the British citizens resident in Argentina were returning to their homeland, Great Britain sent the largest war fleet mobilised since the Second World War. On 25 April a British commando attacked and occupied the Georgias Islands, the initial source of the conflict. The Argentine commander of the area, Lieutenant Alfredo Astiz, surrendered without shooting a single gunshot, and the photograph of his surrender went around the world, thus allowing him to be recognised as one of the major torturers of the ESMA (Escuela de Mecánica de la Armada/The Navy's Mechanics' School), which led to a series of international trials which culminated in his conviction in France in 1995.

Although Argentina undertook Air Force actions of great importance, such as the sinking of the troop carrier *HMS Sheffield*, the British submarine *Conqueror* sank the battleship ARA *General Belgrano* during the peace negotiations undertaken by the Peruvian president Fernando Belaunde Terry, which had finally been accepted by the Military Junta. On 7 May the United Nations initiated peace negotiations, whilst the Argentine forces continued fighting. Margaret Thatcher rejected the "ceasefire" demanded by the UN, stating that a peace agreement with the military was unacceptable, and rejecting the peace proposal taken to London by the UN Secretary Javier Pérez de Cuéllar.

On 28 May the Second Battalion of Parachutists took Port Darwin and Goose Green in the most terrible ground battle of the war. In June, the battles of Mount Longdon, Mount Harriet and Mount Tumbledown marked the British advance. Finally, 14 June, General Menéndez signed the Rendition Act, in which the word "unconditional" appears crossed out, but it was never published by the Argentine's media. On 20 June, the British officially declared an end to hostilities. The immediate consequences of the surrender were the accelerated fall of General Galtieri, who had led the war adventure, whereas Margaret Thatcher was re-elected Prime Minister.[4]

Memory as intimate chronicle twenty years on
At the cessation of the conflict, the Military Junta issued only an extremely succinct communiqué: "The combat in the Malvinas-Falklands has ceased". This left the issue of surrender – news of which was never published in any Argentine communication media – in a semantic vagueness. It is only now that, thanks to the British archives, the last negotiations' reports are starting to get published. "The first thing that I established – General Menéndez recalls – was the issue about the flags. It was a very tense situation. I said to Colonel Rose – who had come to – that before we started, I proposed that if – as they said – the Argentines had fought courageously and bravely, we had the right to return with our war flags. And it was granted to us" (*Clarín*, 15 June 2002, "La ultima negociación" ["The last negotiation"]).

The interpretation of the experience recounted by Menéndez, in the long interview he gave to *Clarín* on the occasion of the anniversary, is extraordinary. He states that, instead of stopping the conflict that had taken place as a result of the presence of merchant ships in the Georgias Islands which initiated the escalation of hostilities, he decided to occupy the Falklands-Malvinas on the basis of a surprise attack. General Menéndez says, "There was a huge rush with problems of military and strategic equipment. The plans covered only the occupation and five more days, the rest had not been planned" (*Clarín*, 15 June 2002, "La guerra no estaba prevista y empezamos a

---

[4] *L'Unità*, 3 April 2002, Paolo di Motoli, "Falkland: suicidio di una dittatura".

Conclusion: Constructing Memory

improvisar" ["The war had not been planned, so we started to improvise"]). The statements of the General – who defended Port Stanley as much as he could – show the lack of a thorough strategic plan as to what to do with the islands once occupied, and points out General Galtieri's and the Junta's irresponsibility in conducting the war, in relation to the setting up of the necessary infrastructure – landing runways, and also bakeries or toilets – but above all, in the preparations for how the war might develop. For instance, the Junta planned an amphibious and not a beachhead landing, such as the one which was set up in San Carlos.

"The air combat – Menéndez continues – was very difficult; beyond the courage and braveness of our pilots, it was impossible because of the material that the Americans had provided to the British, such as the Sidewinder or the British cannon 105 or the target sensor and direction guided systems of the British artillery [...], by the 14th we didn't any longer have response capacity." To the journalist's question of whether he had questioned this improvisation, he replies:

> "There were things that were demanded, but which could not be fulfilled, even if one wanted to [...] Moore had eighty generals of the British General Staff, I had only five [...]. When the British disembarked on the 21st of May in San Carlos I realised that the beachhead was steady. What could be done from the continent? – he wonders. They should have used the fleet but Chile was there. General Guglialmeli once said to me that it was a mistake to face a conflict against the British without having solved the territorial disagreement with Chile. The fact is that there is a moment in which I say, 'Not one more. Not one more single Argentine dead.' We fought on the nights of the 11th and 12th, and ferociously, on the nights of the 13th and 14th, but on the morning of the 14th no reinforcements from the continent arrived [...]. I had the hope that the UN resolution 502 was accepted, which positioned Argentina as the aggressor but also imposed a suspension of hostilities and this was what I let Galtieri know, but he replied, 'I cannot do what you are asking me to do.' And I told him: 'General, if I can't expect anything from you, I don't know what will happen to the Malvinas-Falklands garrison tonight.' The surrender was the toughest decision in my life."

The defeat marked the beginning of the end of the military government. The regime, which had initiated proceedings in 1976, was hounded by the consequences of the neo-liberal model that Economy

Minister José Alfredo Martínez de Hoz had started to implement, and by civil protests that articulated economic discontent with human rights demands. "Peace, bread and jobs" was the slogan of the gigantic first demonstration held on 31 March – just a few hours before the Argentine disembarkartion – which ended in police repression and the imprisonment of the main workers' leaders who had not yet disappeared.

Classed as "surprising" and "an audacity of the military government" (*Clarín* editorial, 2 April 2002, "Twenty years after Malvinas"), this war that confronted, in the middle of the Cold War, the main strategic ally of the United States, with a country belonging to the Washington orbit, found support from the population and solidarity demonstrations in the rest of Latin America. The causes of the defeat, apart from the obvious difference in military power, have also to do with the international and diplomatic reading of the situation, according to which a democratic country was attacked by a military dictatorship that was suspected of serious human rights violations. Also, they had to do with the weakness of the United Nations in managing the crises properly and in intervening in the conflict, which is a recurrent and current weakness, as observed in its management of the situations in the Iraq War, and the Iran and North Korea atomic weapons conflicts during the late nineties. By refusing to comply with resolution 502, Argentina clearly positioned itself as the aggressor country and the United States refused to endorse the application of the TIAR (Inter-American Treaty of Mutual Assistance). The military failure and the evidence of political manipulation precipitated the fall of the dictatorship, to the extent that, immediately after the conflict had finished, a slow but steady transition to democracy began (Escudero Chauvel, 2002a).

The Role of the Media

From the media construction viewpoint, the "war story" tone recurs in 2002 and 2007, on the occasion of the anniversary of the twenty and twenty-five year anniversaries of the Argentine surrender. The main national newspapers' enunciative positions did not vary their way of presenting their headlines. On the one hand, *La Nación*'s headline was: "Twenty Years After the Malvinas War", positioning itself at the site of History, setting itself apart from the facts that it can now analyse, precisely because of the distance made possible by historical discourse. *Clarín*, on the other hand, repeats the same enunciative position that it assumed throughout the conflict, now with the headline: "You have shown your courage and it's time now to avoid more casualties; we

Conclusion: Constructing Memory

offer to you surrender", reproducing – by using direct speech – British Captain Rod Bell's statement. The article – full of details about this British man who spoke Spanish and was in charge of establishing the first contacts by using the frequency of the British medical radio station, which was always open during the conflict – explains how Bell broadcast on 14 June at 9am, "with a Central American accent because he was brought up in Costa Rica", that "it's not worth carrying on fighting. Argentine honour has been proven. They have shown their worth. It's time to stop the fight and to avoid more casualties. We offer to initiate surrender talks with you. You have until 1pm" (*La Nación*, 14 June 2002; *Clarín*, 14 June 2002).

From the viewpoint of a theory of stable media formats and of the strength and persistence of this type of narrative, it is pertinent to note that this story has remained unchanged for practically twenty-five years. The beginning of the news item with which *Clarín* commemorates the war is not very different from that of a TV thriller: "When Jeremy Moore, chief of the British troops, had it confirmed that the entry of his men into Puerto Argentino (*sic*) was assured, he decided that it was time to ask the enemy for their surrender." History becomes a fictional story, and the tone admonitory, confronting the *de facto* president who had led Argentina to war and caused thousands of Argentines to disappear.

If the news media during the war – and even under the censorship and information blackout conditions that were dominant in that period – fulfilled their role, twenty-five years on, they display goodwill in the writing of History as a collection of trivial anecdotes in which the war was the result of an act of pure madness without any apparent cause, a *deus ex machina* which, once set in motion, it was impossible to stop.

The last dialogue between General Menéndez and General Galtieri, in which the former asked the latter strategically to accept resolution 502, and the general-president responds, "We have to get our soldiers out of the ditches, we have to counterattack", highlights the absurdity of this character, but it also reveals the tragedy of the war: the inevitable absence, in the authoritarian military ideology, of a strategic mind, that is to say, of dynamic and flexible thinking. The last order received by Menéndez was a "prohibition on accepting any conditions which may imply a political compromise for the country, in particular, resolution 502", in Galtieri's own words (*Clarín*, 14 June 2002). The surrender conditions we know only now: the Argentines requested, apart from keeping their flags, that the officers could keep their guns. This latter condition had hitherto no precedent in previous surrenders and speaks of both the British flexibility and of their haste to sign the agreement, as well as the fear that the Argentine officers had of their own troops' reaction in the face of the surrender (*Clarín*, 14 June 2002).

The British condition, for its part, was that the name "Malvinas" had to be banned from official documents, and they also asked that the Argentine Air Force ceased attacking them any more, their fear being that the naval air force might continue fighting after the surrender. The last conversations between the officers from both countries confirms the idea that war is at heart a kind of bloody conversation: whilst the British were surprised by the strength of the air attacks, the Argentines were asking why they had taken Darwin, considering it as not of strategic importance. The newspapers reports tell us that these conversations took place "while having tea". This confirms Erwing Goffman's pertinent distinction between the *scene* and its *backstage* in the accomplishment of an interaction of the "machination" type: after more than two hours of sitting at the same table, the two up-to-that-point antagonistic sides showed themselves in their professional role, that of soldiers talking about the technical job they had just done together, without having met each other before.

Conclusions

A diplomatic settlement was never possible because the equation "aggressor military dictatorship" did not allow any honourable negotiation on the British side. And that was undoubtedly a fundamental lesson for Argentine diplomacy: nobody would acknowledge the legitimate claims of an illegitimate government, and even less so its methodology. Argentina, in turn, had to pay her "challenge" to a NATO power with an exemplary punishment: a) Argentine military men ceased to be "peaceful" in foreign affairs and deadly in home affairs, to become an unpredictable threat for the allies of their own bloc; b) the Latin American dictatorships, which had been the hegemonic form of government in the subcontinent during the 1970s began one after the other (Brazil, Chile, Peru, Ecuador) to collapse But in Argentina this process reached unprecedented dimensions, because of the popular fervour that the war produced, or because of her soldiers' very resistance in the islands: it irreversibly disabled the military leadership in the eyes of Argentine society, civil society started to accept the tragedy of the *disappeared*, a new space for critical and judicial revision began to emerge, and the public sphere was filled as never before with the atrocities perpetrated by the dictatorship in the domestic arena, which culminated – once democracy had returned – with the 1985 Juntas Trials and with the Rattenbach Commission peer Trial of the same period. The synthetic formulation

Conclusion: Constructing Memory

of all this was undoubtedly the famous slogan that began to circulate at the end of the war, as an echo and a response to the redeeming military slogans: "The Malvinas are Argentinean, and so too are the *disappeared*."

Bibliography

Adams, V. (1986). *The media and the Falklands campaign.* London: Sage.
Barthes, R. 1984 [1967]. *Essais Critiques n°4. Le bruissement de la langue.* Paris: Seuil.
Beach, P. J. 1983. "The Anglo-argentine dispute over title to the Falklands Islands: Changing British Perceptions on Sovereignty Since 1910". *Millenium: Journal of International Studies* 12, 1 (Spring), 6-24.
Carodoso, R. O., Van der Kooy, E., Kirschbaum,R. 1983. *Malvinas, la trama secreta.* Buenos Aires: Sudamericana.
Eco, U. 1979. *Lector in fabula.* Milano: Bompiani
____ 1990. *I limiti dell'interpretazione.* Milano: Bompiani.
____ 1994. *Sei passegiate nei boschi dei mondi narrativi.* Milano: Bompiani.
Escudero Chauvel, L. 1996. *Malvinas: el gran relato. Fuentes y rumores en la informacion de guerra.* Barcelona: Gedisa.
____ 2007. "Argentina Media in the Malvinas-Falklands conflict." In García Quiroga, D. and Seear, M. (eds.). 2009. *Hors de Combat. The Falklands-Malvinas Conflict in Retrospect.* Nottingham: Critical, Cultural and Communications Press, 99-109.
Fishman, M. 1980. *Manufacturing the News* (Austin: University of Texas Press).
Freedman, L. 2005. *The Official History of the Falklands Campaign: Vol. II – War and Diplomacy.* London: Routledge.
Gamba, V. 1986. *El peon de la reina.* Buenos Aires: Sudamericana.
García Quiroga, D., and Seear, M. 2007. *Hors de Combat: The Falklands-Malvinas Conflict Twenty-Fiove Years On.* Nottingham: Critical, Cultural and Communications Press.
Gavshon, A. and Rice, D. 1984. *The Sinking of the Belgrano.* London: Secker and Warburg.
Glasgow University Media Group. 1985. *War and Peace News.* Milton Keynes: Open University.
Hanrahan, B. and Fox, R. 1982. *I counted them all out and I counted them all back again.* London: BBC.
Harris, P. 1983. *Gotcha! The media, the government and the Falklands crisis.* London: Faber and Faber.
Hastings, M., and Jenkins, S. 1983. *The Battle of the Falklands.* London: Pan.
Holland, P. 1982. "Public opinion, popular press and the organization of ideas". *Falklands, whose crisis?* London: Latin American Bureau Special Brief.
Hooper, R. A. 1982. *The military and the media.* London: Aldershot

Gower.
House of Commons Defence Committee. 1982. *The handling of press and public information during the Falklands conflict* (London: HMSO, 2 vols.).
Joffre, O. L., and Aguiar, F. R. 1987. *La defensa de Puerto Argentino*. Buenos Aires: Sudamericana.
Kapferer, J. N. 1987. *Rumeurs*. Paris: Seuil.
Kirschbaum, R. 1983. *Malvinas, la trama secreta*. Buenos Aires: Sudamericana.
Lester, M. 1980. "Generating newsworthiness: the interpretative construction of public events". *American Sociological Review* 45 (December), 984-94.
Lorenz, F. 2006. *Las guerras por Malvinas*. Buenos Aires: Sudamericana.
Marletti, C. 1984. *Media e politica*. (Milan: Angeli).
McGuirk, B. 2007. *Falklands- Malvinas. An Unfinished Business*. Seattle: New Ventures.
Molotch, H. and Lester, M. 1974. "News as purposive behavior: on the strategic use of routine events, accidents and scandals", *American Sociological Review* 39 (February), 101-12.
Moro, R. 1985. *La guerra inaudita*. Buenos Aires: Pleamar.
Morrison, D. E., and Tumber, H. 1988. *Journalists at War: Dynamics of News Reporting During the Falklands Conflict*. London: Sage.
N Revista de Cultura no. 183. (March 2007). *A 25 años de la guerra de las Malvinas*.
Neguine, R. 1989. *Politics and the mass media in Britain*. London: Routledge.
Nott, J. 2002. *Here Today, Gone Tomorrow*. London: Politicos.
Robacio, C. H. Contralmirante. (2004). *Desde el frente. Batallon de Infanteria de Marina n°5*. Buenos Aires: Talleres Gráficos Tiara.
Falkland Islands Review: Report of a Committee of Privy Counsellors. Chmn. Lord Franks (Command 8787) [Franks Report]. 1983. London: HMSO.
Royal Institute for International Affairs. 1982. *The Falklands Island dispute: international dimensions*. London: Royal Institute for International Affairs.
Ruiz Moreno, I. J. 1986. *Comandos en Acción*. Buenos Aires: Emecé.
Schoenfeld, M. 1982. *La guerra austral*. Buenos Aires: Editorial Desafío Editores.
Seear, M. 2003. *With the Gurkhas in the Falklands: A War Journal*. Barnsley: Pen and Sword Books.
Seear, M. 2012. *Return to Tumbledown: the Falklands-Malvinas War Revisited*. Nottingham: Critical, Cultural and Communications Press.
Thatcher, M. [1993] 2011. *The Downing Street Years*. London:

HarperCollins.
Thompson, J. 1985. *No picnic*. London: Secker and Warburg
Tuchman, G. 1978. *Making the News*. New York: Free Press.
Van Sant Hall, M. 1983. *Argentine policy in the Falklands War: the Political Results*. Newport, CT: US Naval War College.
Verbitsky. H. 1984. *La ultima batalla de la Tercera Guerra Mundial*. Buenos Aires: Sudamericana.
Wilhoit, G. (ed.). 1981 *Mass Media Communication Review Yearbook.*, vol. 2. London: Sage.

INDEX

Adams, V., 29-30, 122, 124, 137, 140, 145, 148, 153-6, 184
Admiralty, the, 109
AFP, 51, 61, 83, 85, 87, 90-1, 96, 98, 100, 102, 104-5, 109-110, 133
Aguiar, F. R., 158-60, 168-70, 173, 185
Alfonsín, R., 21, 45, 163, 175
Alfredo, J., 4, 20, 122, 131, 133-4, 177, 180
Anaya, Admiral J. I., 106, 135, 176
ARA General Belgrano, 4, 32, 69, 88, 116, 141-4, 146, 149-50, 152-6, 175, 177, 184
ARA Piedrabuena, 141
Argentine Embassy, 8, 46, 74, 76, 133
Astiz, A., 4, 122, 125, 128, 131, 133-5, 177
ATC, 31
Baltiérrez, R., 62, 137, 142
Barthes, R., 23-4, 184
BBC, 21, 24, 30, 64, 73, 137, 148, 170, 185
Belaunde T. F., 139, 141, 148-9, 177
Bell, Captain R., 181
Bignone, E., 16, 175
Bonzo, Captain H., 141
Brazil, 61, 111, 183
Carballo, Captain P., 139
Cardoso, O. R., 8, 59, 63-4, 68, 122, 125, 133, 141, 149-50, 156, 159, 165, 168-70, 173
Carrington, Lord, 73, 119
Catholic Church, 47, 167

CBS, 63, 137
Cesareo, G., 50-1
CGT (Confederación General de los Trabajadores), 68
Channel 13, 31
Channel 7, 31
Chile, 61, 89, 167, 179, 183
Clarín, 9, 10, 17, 30, 33-5, 40, 43-4, 48-9, 51, 56, 58-64, 67, 69-72, 74, 76-7, 81-7, 89-91, 93-4, 96-111, 113-14, 117-18, 121-6, 128-9, 131-4, 137-8, 142-4, 150-2, 160-73, 175, 178, 180-2
Costa Rica, 181
Daily Mail, The, 93
Daily Mirror, The, 93
Daily Record, The, 10, 111
Daily Star, The, 93
Daily Telegraph, The, 9, 86, 98
Dalyell, T., 89, 145
de Hoz, M., 180
di Motoli, P., 178
Dozo, Brigadier L., 106, 171
Eco, U., 3, 7, 9, 27, 97, 99, 101, 106-7, 184
Editorial Abril, 35
Editorial Perfil, 35
Escribano, J. C., 175
Escudero Chauvel, L., 1, 2, 9, 180, 184
ESMA (Escuela de Mecanica de la Armada), 177
Exocet missiles, 150-1, 155
Fabbri, P., 7
Fallaci, O., 169
Faslane, 111
Financial Times, The, 69, 93
Foreign and Commonwealth Office (UK), 74

Fox, R., 140, 185
Franks Report, 75, 119, 186
Freedman, Sir L., 29, 184
Frondizi, A., 45
Galtieri, General F., 16, 56, 71, 75, 82-3, 106, 165-6, 168-9, 172-4, 177, 179, 182
Gamba, V., 29, 132, 137, 184
Gans, H., 49-50, 59
Gavshon, A., 89, 137, 139, 141, 149-50, 159, 184
Gente y la Actualidad, 35, 129, 131, 135, 139
Georgias Islands, 27-8, 30, 36, 63, 70, 75, 111, 116, 119, 121, 124, 126, 128, 130-1, 133-4
Gibraltar, 96, 98, 104-6, 114
Glasgow University Media Group, 17, 29, 65, 140, 145-6, 148, 153, 155-6, 184
Goffman, E., 50, 182
Grice, J., 94
Guardian, The, 94, 146
Haig, A. (American Secretary of State), 46, 63, 91-3, 104, 106-7, 109-11, 117, 139, 176
Hanrahan, B., 24, 140, 185
Harrier, 24, 137-8, 147, 151-2
Harris, P., 29, 185
Hastings, M., 17, 68, 89, 93-4, 116, 121-2, 137, 141, 144, 150, 152, 158, 160, 168-9, 170, 185
Hill, N., 87
HMS Conqueror, 116, 122, 141, 147, 149, 177
HMS Hermes, 108, 135, 138-9, 147
HMS Invincible, 64, 90, 154
HMS Sheffield, 4, 88, 149-56, 177
HMS Splendid, 32, 105, 115-17
Holland, P., 29, 61, 185
House of Commons, 29, 102, 105, 157, 185
human rights, 7, 134, 168, 176, 180
Hunt, Governor R., 86
International Institute for Strategic Studies, 98
Iraq, 55, 180
IRN, 30
Isnard, J., 104
ITN, 30, 145-6, 148, 155
ITV, 30, 96
Jenkins, S., 17, 68, 89, 93-4, 116, 121-2, 137, 141, 144, 150, 152, 158, 160, 168-70, 185
Joffre, O. L., 158-60, 168-70, 173, 185
Jukic, Lieutenant A., 138-9
La Nación, 30, 32-6, 48-51, 58-63, 67, 71-4, 76, 81-3, 85-6, 90-1, 93-4, 108, 121-3, 127, 130, 132, 134, 139, 142-3, 144, 150-2, 160-7, 171-3, 175,181
La Prensa, 122, 126-8, 132, 143, 157
La Semana y Usted, 35
Le Monde, 10, 104, 152, 175
Lepri, S., 51
Lester, M., 26, 41-2, 185
Lewin, Admiral Sir L., 141, 145-6
Lombardo, Admiral J., 69
Luce, R., 82
Maiorano, Commodore H., 138-9
Mar del Plata, 100, 102-4
Mayor, Commodore S., 98,

Index

121, 166
McGuirk, B., 7, 185
Méndez, N. C., 46, 71-2, 74-5, 91, 106, 127, 157, 172, 175
Menéndez, General B. M., 71, 168-72, 176-9, 181-2
Military Junta, 16, 43, 45, 59, 62-3, 68, 70, 82, 93, 106, 117, 124-5, 128-9, 131, 137, 146, 164, 166, 167, 170, 173-4, 177-8
Mirage(s), 151
Mitre, 32, 60, 127
Molteni, A., 8, 46, 74, 76, 164
Montevideo, 107, 132-3, 176
Moore, General J., 170, 172, 179, 181
Moro, O., 121-2, 130-1, 137, 142, 150, 158, 168, 170, 185
Morrison, D., 29, 55, 154, 185
Mount Harriet, 158, 177
Mount Longdon, 158, 177
Mount Tumbledown, 29, 158, 166, 177, 186
NATO, 86, 114, 174, 183
News at Ten, 30
North Korea, 180
Nott, J. (British Defence Minister), 73-4, 86, 99, 101-2, 112-13, 123, 145-6, 157, 186
Observer, The, 24, 93
Palermo Park, 166
Panorama, 30
Pérez de Cuéllar, J., 156, 177
Plaza de Mayo, 20, 68-9, 71, 173
Plymouth, 85, 121
Pope John Paul II, 31, 47, 82, 165-8
Port Stanley, 70, 76-7, 86, 100, 138, 158, 161-2, 164, 171-2, 175, 178
Portsmouth, 103, 106
Portugal, 176
Púcara, 138-9
Radio, 30, 32
Rattenbach Commission, 135, 183
Reagan, R. (US President), 46, 75-6, 84, 175
Rice, D., 89, 137, 139, 141, 149-50, 159, 184
Robacio, Captain C. H., 7, 29, 186
Ros, E., 164
Rose, Colonel, 178
Royal Navy, 98, 104, 155
Ruiz Moreno, I., 122, 137, 158-9, 168-9, 186
Salt, S., 150
Searle, J., 119
Second Battalion of Parachutists, 177
Secret Service, 86
Seear, Major M., 7, 29, 184, 186
Seear, Major Mike, 184
self-determination, 176
Sergeant, J. C., 17, 29-30
Sidewinder missiles, 179
South Atlantic Council, 19
Southern Sandwich Islands, 70
Spain, 61, 96, 160, 164, 176
Submarine(s), 4, 10-11, 96
Suez Canal, 90, 92
Sun, The, 93, 147
Sunday Times, The, 17, 93, 147
Super Etendard, 149, 151-2, 155
Task Force, 9-10, 17, 65, 85, 90-3, 102, 106, 115, 118, 121, 145-8, 152-4, 175
TELAM, 51, 60-2, 90, 110,

134, 138-9, 143
Terragno, R., 103
Thatcher, M. (British Prime Minister), 64, 75, 83, 84, 87, 102, 106, 112, 123, 144, 149-50, 153, 165, 169, 177-8, 186
TIAR (Inter-American Defence Treaty), 16, 137, 180
Times, The, 86, 94, 104-5, 147, 169
Tuchman, G., 26, 41-2, 51-2, 54, 59, 88, 186
Tumber, H., 29, 55, 154, 185
TV Eye, 30

Union Jack, 73
United Nations, 17, 45-6, 60, 72, 104, 109, 143, 156-7, 164, 176-7, 180
University of Nottingham, 184
UPI, 51, 62, 83, 85, 86-7, 102, 110
Ushuaia, 143
Van der Kooy, E., 184
Vulcan, 140
Washington Post, The, 91, 137, 147
Wilhoit, G., 43, 186
Wolf, M., 112, 155
Wreford-Brown, C., 141

www.ingramcontent.com/pod-product-compliance
Lightning Source LLC
Chambersburg PA
CBHW051758040426
42446CB00007B/429